The Magic of Wolves

The Magic of Wolves

Robin Herne

MOON
BOOKS

Winchester, UK
Washington, USA

JOHN HUNT PUBLISHING

First published by Moon Books, 2024
Moon Books is an imprint of John Hunt Publishing Ltd., No. 3 East Street, Alresford
Hampshire SO24 9EE, UK
office@jhpbooks.net
www.johnhuntpublishing.com
www.moon-books.net

For distributor details and how to order please visit the 'Ordering' section on our website.

ISBN: 978 1 80341 106 4
978 1 80341 107 1 (ebook)
Library of Congress Control Number: 2022945808

A CIP catalogue record for this book is available from the British Library.

Design: Lapiz Digital Services

UK: Printed and bound by CPI Group (UK) Ltd, Croydon, CR0 4YY
Printed in North America by CPI GPS partners

We operate a distinctive and ethical publishing philosophy in
all areas of our business, from our global network of authors to
production and worldwide distribution.

Contents

This book is dedicated to:

The staff and volunteers at the UK Wolf Trust for looking after the wolves and enabling many happy visits to walk with the lupines over the years;

My ancient Jack Russell, Cafall, who died during the writing of this book – run wild;

Bronntanas, an abandoned Malamute who arrived in my life (thanks to an intervention by a student) at a time when we both needed rescuing.

Introduction

For many years I went on an annual pilgrimage to the Wolf Sanctuary in Reading to see their resident wolves and, under the supervision of their experienced volunteers, walk through the local woods in the wake of the wolf pack. Whilst they no longer do open visits, the memories will remain with me for life of feeling a wolf's pelt beneath my fingers, being held captive by a pair of yellow eyes just inches from me, or being recognised by a wolf even after twelve months, of having a wet nose snuffling in my ear. There is something primal about sitting with a creature powerful enough to kill me with one snap of its jaws which nonetheless chooses to show affection and curiosity instead.

The sound of a chorus ululating a few feet away raises hairs on the back of the neck and doubtless sends shivers all the way down the ancestral line to some distant forebear walking home through the woods at dusk after a day of toil and hearing that exact same song. Some of my ancestors may well have been utterly terrified by it, but others were hopefully as mesmerised as I was.

The aim of this book, which forms part of a wider series by assorted authors each looking at the magical lore connected to a different species, is to give the reader an overarching grasp of global mythology and folklore, connecting it to a bedrock of zoology, history, culture, and spirituality. Practically all societies at some point in history have sought mystical interaction with the animals on which they depended or which they greatly admired. This book will offer some guidance to the reader on potential ways to communicate with wolves as part of ritual practice.

Wolves the world over are a marginalised species, hunted and hated with impunity. If the reader of this book has any sympathy whatsoever for our lupine kin, then I can but encourage them (if they do not do so already) to support wolf conservation efforts. There are varied ways in which this can be done – donations to relevant causes, pressuring politicians to change laws, gently educating the wider public who may fear wolves (though avoid hectoring people, few things alienate from a cause more quickly), presenting positive images of wolves through the arts etc. When it comes to the latter, this book is one of my contributions in this direction, though I suspect it may be mostly preaching to the choir.

The chapters of this book guide the reader across various European cultures and makes forays into Egypt, India, China and Japan. The book makes no claim to be an exhaustive account of wolf mythology and folklore, so there may well be occasions where some readers find themselves wondering why some story or concept they are familiar with has not appeared. In order to cover even half the stories out there, it would need to be three times longer than it is!

During the planning stage for this book, I thought about the many stories found both amongst the native peoples of the Americas and also the more recent folktales of modern Americans, but the limitations of word count when faced with such an extensive body of lore made this impossible to do any justice to. It is, I think, ultimately worthy of an entire book just on that landmass alone. Whilst, thanks to advances in DNA research, zoologists have only recently come to the conclusion that wolves are more widespread in Africa than they previously realised, there is a large body of folklore – again, too much to cover in this slim volume.

As well as listing lore, some interpretations of what they mean and how they can inform modern audiences are offered, drawing on a variety of perspectives. It is hoped that these will stimulate reflection and discussion.

A mountain with a wolf on it stands a little higher.

Russian proverb

Chapter 1

Sons of the Countryside

One of the old Scots Gaelic names for a wolf is *mactire*, which translates as 'son of the countryside'. During the later decades of the 20th century wolves became romantic emblems of the wilderness in popular western thought. This was powerfully captured in the cinematography of the 1990 film *Dances with Wolves* in which Kevin Costner plays the troubled army lieutenant John Dunbar. Posted to a lonely fort, if such it can be called, on the vast plains of Tennessee he comes to befriend both the local Lakota community and a wolf, with whom the Native Americans see him playing. Based on a book from 1988, the film captures the seeming death of a culture that is presented as at-one with the natural world. The encroaching army and the government they serve despise the natives as much as they hate the wolves, and regard nature as simply a resource to exploit and eventually build over. Book and film alike were a paean to the beauties of the vast open spaces and the humans and other creatures that embraced them.

Whilst the film has a decided rosy tint to it, earlier generations – including the actual colonisers of the 1860s – also saw wolves and nature as synonymous, albeit in a negative way. Wolves are red in tooth and claw and so is Mother Nature. It tends to be mostly comfortable townies that imagine that a life without running water, central heating, penicillin, or a regular food supply was somehow akin to a jolly weekend glamping. The vast majority of people living in rural environments two centuries or more ago (and for a great many people still today) were fully aware that the wilderness was a dangerous place full of threats to life and limb. Whilst recorded wolf attacks on humans are exceedingly rare, threats to livestock (and therefore vital food supplies) did happen and so the hunger of the lupine predators must have been genuinely frightening. To those for whom the wilderness beyond the bounds of village or town were, or still are, disturbing and dangerous places the wolf has so often served as both visual and auditory reminder of those risks.

Before we immerse ourselves in the narrative realms of mythology and legend, it seems suitable to lay some zoological groundwork with a few facts and figures about the animals under focus. The focus of this chapter will be to address these issues. The global wolf population has declined over the centuries due to excessive hunting, environmental degradation, and deliberate attempts at genocide. In some areas the numbers are gradually improving, mainly as a result of increased legal protections and concerted conservation work. In the final chapter the issue of conservation and what can be done to aid wolf survival will be considered.

Modern wolves are descendants of the dire wolf (*Aenocyon dirus*), which lived during the Late Pleistocene and early Holocene. The dire was similar in appearance to the modern species, though bigger and heavier set at around 150 pounds (68 kilogrammes) for the larger males. They died out around 9,500 years ago, prowling what would eventually become North America though they could be found all the way across to north-eastern China. Their presence in other regions cannot be refuted, but is yet to be supported by the fossil record. Human culture was developing during the last few centuries of the dire wolves' existence, with farming and smelting in their formative stages. It does not require a belief in race memory to accept that storytellers would spin accounts about massive wolves spotted in the shadows around the camp, tales which became ever more gruesome with each telling. Ancient accounts of dire wolves may well form the basis for some of the darker myths and legends of monstrous lupines that will be explored in later chapters. The domestication process for the smaller types of wolves (dire wolves do not appear to have been tamed) began any time between 14,000 and 29,000 years ago, eventually resulting in the dogs that are now to be found on every continent on the planet. Household dogs can be thought of rather as distant cousins of their wild kin. The tension between wild and tame is something that has been explored in many myths and legends.

Wolves were once widespread from Europe and across to North America. The native species on these continents is the grey or timber wolf (*Canis lupus*). Whilst the name timber conjures up images of forests, this species of wolf adapts itself to many different environments. In the wild they average a lifespan of around 8 years, but some individuals have been noted to last as long as 13 years. This lifespan is comparable to that of many breeds of domestic dog. Male timber wolves are just over 6.5 feet from nose to tail (2 metres). An adult male weighs around 100 pounds (45 kilogrammes) though that obviously depends on available diet. Female wolves are around four-fifths the size of the males (about 80 pounds or 36 kilogrammes). The size of both sexes varies, with the larger breeds in the northern regions of their spread and the smaller ones at the southern zones. The colour of pelts varies from black through assorted shades of grey to silvery white. A reddish-tan colour can also be found in some regions. Whilst not exactly camouflaged, their pelts do blend into the environment which improves the capacity to sneak up on prey as well as avoid hostile forces. The timber wolf has a number of subspecies that have adapted to certain locations. Zoological classification is not a wholly straightforward matter and there is some dispute as to the number of subspecies. This chapter will focus on some of the more commonly agreed upon subspecies. Tragically, many subspecies have already gone extinct.

Wolves are renowned hunters; greys are able to run at 37 miles (60 km) per hour and traverse vast distances in a day. A hunting territory can be anything up to 1,200 square miles (3,000 square kilometres), though usually decidedly smaller. Within this terrain wolves will eat nigh on any herbivorous mammal or, in some regions, fresh water fish that does not getaway fast enough. Zoologists note that wolves mainly predate on prey animals that are elderly, unwell or injured in some way, or too young to attain the full mobility of healthy adulthood. Evolutionary theory might regard this as thinning the herd of its weaker members, ultimately strengthening the surviving herd. As well as hunting, wolves will also consume carrion and, in areas close to human occupancy, have been seen rummaging through dustbins. The colloquialism of wolfing down food comes from the lupine capacity to consume large quantities of meat in one sitting. Wolves have been witnessed devouring up to 20 pounds (9 kilogrammes) in a single meal. Whether they get indigestion afterwards is another question entirely.

A pack can be anything from a half a dozen all the way up to two dozen if food supplies are sufficient. Smaller packs are more common. Each group is based around a breeding pair (commonly referred to as the alpha male and alpha female, though many zoologists no longer use such terms) and the generations of their children. Wolves are intensely social animals. Alphas are the prime breeding pair and appear to coordinate activities like hunting. Though not members of the pack, it is worth noting that wolves maintain social relations with ravens. Zoologists have observed large gatherings of ravens (the collective noun is an unkindness) making an awful lot of noise when they find the carcass of a deer or some other unfortunate herbivore. The cawing attracts wolves (and sometimes other predators) who rip the dead body apart. The wolves gain a free meal and the ravens are better able to consume the smaller scraps of shredded flesh than they are the original intact body. More than simply sharing food resources, naturalists have frequently noticed ravens and young wolves playing games with each other – teasing and chasing each other. Derek Ratcliffe (1997) and other conservationists have noted that various types of covids come to recognise individual human faces and can identify both friends and enemies. If they can pick out particular people there is no reason why they may not be able to do the same with wolves. The Irish goddess Morrigan takes the form of both a carrion crow and a wolf, perhaps reflective of observations made by storytellers or the goddess manifesting through species that have a natural sympathy for each other.

She-wolves gestate for two months, mating season commonly occurring around December and January for timber wolves. Birth occurs between February and April, normally with five or six cubs to a litter. The breeding pair typically hunt out a den, making best use of whatever the environment offers them. The most famous wolf den is the cave in which the outcast Roman twins Romulus and Remus were reared by Lupa. The exact location of the Lupercal, as the cave was called in Latin, was lost for many centuries. Each generation of cubs is looked after by the whole pack, not just the immediate parents – doubtless part of the reason for their success. Practically all wolf species mate for life, though it is normally only the dominant pair in any pack that form a union. Some zoologists have noted partnered wolves appearing to occasionally put it around with other wolves but this seems to be a rarity. Weaning occurs around nine weeks, though sometimes earlier. During the first few months of life the cubs gradually become more independent and migrate from being suckled in the den to becoming more adventurous in the outside world. By autumn the young are normally strong enough to travel across their territories along with the adults. Depending on the availability of food, full size is normally attained within nine months of birth. Sexual maturity pushes the young to seek out mates of their own at around the age of two, sometimes traveling vast distances to find a partner.

Subspecies include the red wolf (*Canis lupus rufus*), so-called because of their colour though some can have black pelts. Nose to tail they range from 54 to 66 inches (138 to 168cm) long, and weighs about 44–82 pounds (20–37 kilograms). Red wolves are actually hybrids of greys and coyotes. On the endangered list, captive-reared red wolves were reintroduced to the Albemarle Peninsula on the coast of North Carolina. They used to range over a wider area before depredations greatly reduced their numbers. Increasing numbers of conservationists are taking the view that the red wolf is not so much a subspecies of the grey as a distinct species in itself. The mating and birthing seasons for red wolves are much the same as for the greys. The eastern states of North America are home to the eastern wolf (*Canis lupus lycaeon*) subspecies. Similar in appearance and size to the grey wolf they also the result of hybridisation with coyotes.

Moving away from the northern continents, the Ethiopian wolf (*Canis simensis*) used to be considered a jackal rather than a wolf. It is found mostly in the higher altitudes of Ethiopia and is also on the endangered list. The taxonomical disputation over whether a particular creature is a wolf or jackal also occurs with the Egyptian jackal (*Canis aureus lupaster*). This creature, closely allied to the Egyptian deity Wepwawet, is listed as a subspecies of the golden jackal. However, molecular evidence suggests it is actually a wolf. As well as Egypt these animals can also be found in Libya, and Ethiopia.

The Arabian wolf (*Canis lupus arabs*) is the smallest and probably leanest of the subspecies weighing in at 40–45 pounds (18–20 kilogrammes). This may be due to the paucity of food in the desert. Its territory has decreased over the years and it is now seldom seen outside of the southern areas of Israel, Oman, Yemen, Jordan, Saudi Arabia and Egypt. The numbers in these regions are minimal, largely as a result of concerted poisoning, shooting and other forms of extermination. They have unusual paws with two fused toes, adapted to traveling the blistering sands and leaving very distinctive prints in the sand. In contrast to timber wolves, the Arabian has a breeding season which stretches from October to November. The females gestate for just over two months, birthing around December and January.

A distinct species of wolf, rather than a subspecies of the timber, is the delightfully peculiar maned wolf (*Chrysocyon brachyurus*). It is a native inhabitant of South America, chiefly found in Paraguay, Bolivia, Brazil, Peru, Uruguay, and Argentina. Maned wolves, having been genetically isolated for quite some time, have the surreal look of foxes on stilts and bear little visual resemblance to the wolves of Europe or North America. Very tall creatures, they stand over 3 feet (just under 1 metre) tall at the shoulder and stretch 4 feet (1.2 metres) from nose to tail. The long legs may give them an evolutionary advantage in peering over the long grasses on the plains. They weigh in at 44-55 pounds (20-25 kilogrammes). There are only a few thousand left in the wild, due to environmental devastation and exposure to canine diseases. Unlike other wolves, they do not live in packs but form life-long monogamous couples that share a 10-mile square territory but only interact during the breeding season between April and June. The window in which breeding can take place is actually very brief, lasting less than a week for both sexes. Outside of that they go their own ways, a relationship which some humans might envy. That said, there is some evidence from zoo studies that the males participate in providing cubs with food so there is some additional contact. Alongside meat their diet includes sugarcane, tubers and fruits, most especially a small red berry called lobeira ("fruit of the wolf"). Those interested in a ritualistic communication with the spirits of the maned wolf might consider these berries as suitable offerings, if they are lucky enough to lay hands to any. Their food sources may partially contribute to the very pungent urine with which they mark territory. Whereas most other wolves famously howl, the maned cousin does not but instead barks and makes raucous roaring sounds. The interested reader who does not live in one of the countries where they are to be found could track down a nature documentary or YouTube (or similar) clip of them communicating. Lifespans in captivity have on rare occasions reached as high as 15 years, though on average are less than half that. How long they last in the wild remains unknown, due to their elusive nature.

Chapter 2

In the Lupercal

For the Ancient Romans the story of the Twins and the She-Wolf was as fundamental to their identity as the Royal Myth was to Egyptian culture. This is the story of Romulus and Remus. Their tale is essentially the tale of the wolf as well. In short, before the eternal City ever existed there stood the small community of Alba Longa. In that distant time Alba Longa was ruled over by the bucolic King Numitor who was more interested in his grape vines than it the usual politicking and ruthless ambition of royalty. The same could not be said of his brother Amulius!

In a tale that has decided echoes to the rivalry between Asur (called Osiris by the Greeks) and his ambitious brother Setekh (Seth), Amulius felt his own posterior better suited to sitting upon a throne and had old Numitor displaced and put under effective house arrest at his villa. This unusually peaceful move may well reflect a deep-rooted aversion to kin slaying. A great many ancient cultures, particularly those with what the anthropologist Ruth Benedict (1989) categorised as shame-based systems, have a somewhat relaxed attitude to killing but under specific conditions. The spilling of familial blood is often considered particularly heinous, even where the murder of a stranger might not elicit so much concern. Such views can often extend to other, non-violent behaviours so that a trader who fleeces a stranger is just good at business, whereas if they were to overcharge or short-change a member of their own kin it would be regarded as contemptible dishonesty. Amulius will not murder his brother, nor kill his niece Rhea Silvia – but he will take steps to ensure that she cannot give birth to some future rival to the stolen throne. To this end, she is relegated to the temple of the Vestal Virgins who are not allowed to know the touch of a man until their service to the goddess is ended in middle age.

The gods do not like to be thwarted, and Mars takes a special interest in the fate of Alba Longa. Whilst the temple of Vesta is forbidden territory to mortal men, the warrior god goes where he pleases. Rhea Silvia falls pregnant, a great scandal for a vestal priestess, and whilst other women in that situation faced a gruesome fate, this particular maiden simply gives birth to twins and returns to her duties. Amulius orders his great-nephews to be taken up by a minion, placed in a basket and cast into the River Tiber. Again, the upstart will not countenance the killing of kin-blood but reasons that, should the babes drown or die of exposure, this is the deed of the river and no fault of his. The river spirit Tiberinus and Mars will not be outdone by the schemes of mortals, and guide the basket downriver to a place of safety where it washes ashore close to the Palatine Hill. There one of the holy creatures of Mars, a wolf, finds the infants and takes the as her own to suckle. This benign beast is Lupa, the she-wolf, whose image adorned countless *vexilla* (the standards carried aloft by a soldier called a *vexillarius* who, where Lupa was depicted on the *vexillum*, wore a wolfskin on their head). Her most famous image is the Capitoline Wolf, which originally was a lone beast until the suckling twins were added in the 15th century.

Along with her mate, Lupercus, and the rest of the pack they nurtured the children for the first few years of their lives until the shepherd Faustulus spotted the feral creatures and took them back to be socialised to human ways in his home. What becomes of the wolf pack after this is not recorded, but the two boys retain their lupine mannerisms for life. The shepherd's wife, Acca Larentia, transforms the feral lads into near-normal humans. The word *lupa* was also used as slang for a prostitute and *lupercal* (wolf-cave) as a euphemism for a brothel, which has led some historians to speculate that Acca Larentia might have had a trade of her own to ply and the story of the discovery of the twins might have been an uncharacteristically coy cover for who actually raised them. The link between sex workers and wolves is based upon the unwarranted view that both have voracious sexual appetites.

Years pass and, according to the Roman writer Livy, one of the lads is captured by an old man, Numitor, who recognises the family resemblance. The tale of Romulus and Remus comes out and their royal identity is established with doubtless a combination of shock and joy. Plutarch has it that the discovery would have been no great surprise to the shepherd, who had always an inkling of who the babies were. The brothers are informed of the perfidy carried out by their great-uncle and, clearly living by lupine standards with no squeamish concern about kin slaying, Amulius meets a sticky end not long after. Numitor is restored to his rightful place, and rules in peace for his remaining years. Eventually Romulus and Remus share the throne jointly, expanding the rule of Alba Longa and the Latin peoples. However, they fall out in a dispute over where to build the eternal city. Romulus wants to found it on the Palatine Hill where the rediscovered wolves' cave is (which becomes a shrine, housing the bones of the long-dead pack). Brother Remus would prefer to build on the Aventine Hill. The fight gets out of hand and turns to murder; with Remus dead the eternal city is named Rome and not Rheims. Such figures cast long shadows and after his own death many years later Romulus was deified as the celestial being sometimes referred to under his own name and sometimes as Quirinus. There is no suggestion that Remus was deified or received worship.

Rome was officially founded on April 21st, a day of celebrations also incorporating the Parilia, when Pales the goddess (though sometimes a god, and sometimes even twins) of shepherds was given her due. It may be a coincidence, but there is an echo between Pales and the figure of Faustulus who presumably would have made sacrifice to her. That Pales sometimes manifests as dual figures and may well link to the Sicilian twin brother Palici deities is also highly suggestive. Titus Pomponius Atticus placed the founding in the year 753BCE but other dates were also circulated such that, ultimately, nobody knew for certain. Modern day followers of the Religio Romana, or pagans with less of a commitment to Rome but a general interest in the culture, might well choose to hold ritual on April 21st that could incorporate communion with Lupa the Wolf Mother.

Speaking of festivities, the Romans marked a festival on February 15th that was so ancient even they were not sure when it had started or quite what it was really about as it predated Rome itself. Livy was of the view that it might have started as a Greek festivity, though it was decidedly Roman in his day. With the rigorous orthopraxy of Rome that stuck to the form even when they were uncertain of the purpose. On this day in the Eternal City two colleges of high-born young priests gathered in the Lupercal. These were the Luperci Quinctiales (devoted to Romulus) and the Luperci Fabiani (followers of Remus) ~ Mark Anthony being one of the more famous members. At least one representative from each college stripped naked and together sacrificed a dog and a goat. They smeared blood on their foreheads, then wiped it off with wool dipped in milk. The men made a show of laughing (it being important to be jovial, in both senses) and wrapped strips of the goat's skinned hide about themselves. A great feast was then held – perhaps involving the remains of the goat. Finally, each of the two men led a group of scantily clad priests around the seven hills to mark the bounds of Rome. Women would line up to be thwacked by the runners with strips of goat skin (it is worth noting that untanned hide is not hard enough to hurt, so this was not a sadomasochistic act!) The belief was that this would improve their chances of pregnancy.

A clear analogy can be drawn between the two priests and the twins, the killing of a herd animal and a herd defender an echo of the feral days living in the Lupercal. Perhaps the early Romans combine older, rural traditions with a celebration of the foundation of the city. This may have been a way of giving honour both to the twins and the wolves who nurtured them. Faunus Lupercus, the alpha male, was one deity associated with this ritual. Scant written mention is made of Lupa but it seems likely she would have been honoured too. Plutarch linked the ceremony to Pan, who has much in common with Faunus.

Lupercalian festivities continued until Pope Gelasius I outlawed them in 494CE. The Church instituted the Purification of the Blessed Virgin. The feast day of St Valentine was added to the calendar two years later. The habit of sending love tokens on this date goes back to at least the 14th century. The Pope's motives in creating the new saint's day are unknown. It may have been to adapt the enthusiasm for Lupercalia to a more socially acceptable pattern, though there isn't much connection between sending soppy love letters and slapping women with bits of dead goat. Some hard-to-substantiate accounts suggest that in Roman-occupied Gaul, at Lupercalia, single women wrote their names on clay tablets and placed them in an earthen jar. Unwed young men then picked out a name at random, and the two were paired off. Depending on which account you accept, this lasted a few hours, a day, or even a year.

Lupercalia poses a challenge for modern Pagans who wish to celebrate it. Clearly most of the activities conducted in Ancient Rome would result in arrest, or prosecution by the RSPCA. Either one must engage in an act of quite distasteful civil disobedience, or find a way of adapting the spirit to a new form. Naked rituals in private might be fun, but the procession could be replaced by a socially-acceptable celebration of Roman culture, e.g. a living history display for the public, or something similar. Though the she-wolf is a significant feature in the story, there is a decidedly masculine feel to Lupercalia, with the men gathering in the cave. Brotherhood could be part of the focus. Hopefully not in the guise of one of those ghastly male-bonding roll-in-the-mud for a mere £500 events that psychobabblers flog. Rather, a chance to think on the importance of male friendship. Whether you get naked or not is another question again. Regardless of that, it could be a useful opportunity for the pagan male to delve into their own psyche. Drinking a toast to brothers, of blood or spirit, might form a good centrepiece to a modernised ceremony.

Amulius deprived his great-nephews of their parents. Mars stepped in and gave them wolf parents. Another aspect that could be reflected upon is the way in which the Gods provide alternatives when we suffer losses in our lives. Or, indeed, how we need to aid those less fortunate than ourselves.

Those who enjoy a bit of consensual thwacking could still do so after the sacrifices have been made. If there are no women present who want to get pregnant, then the concept of the men imparting a blessing using some object sacrificed earlier could be reworked. If not fertility of body, then creativity of mind might be far more desirable. Those wanting to be so blessed could be touched with the item previously dedicated to the Gods. If sufficient numbers of men are present, one group could do the food and the other tend to an activity connected to the blessing, thus maintaining the practice of the two priestly bands. The process of taking old habits and finding new expressions for them is one common to pagan reconstructionists of all traditions. Considerably creativity is needed, but it is still possible to retain the spirit of the old in the form of the new ~ if the wolf howls to you.

Mars' connection to wolves is also reinforced by various statues and other imagery from around the Empire. Livy recounts a supposedly true story in his 'History of Rome' about a battle between Roman soldiers and Gaulish warriors. This clash of forces took place in the third century BCE. After much shenanigans involving traitors in the camp of the Gauls selling battle plans to the Romans, the two powers came to slaughter each other. The war raged for three days until a strange incident was witnessed in the field at either end of which the enemies were gathered. As the warriors watched, a wolf chased a deer down from the mountains. In an unexpected turn, the two animals then split mid-field to run in opposite directions. The deer veered off towards the Gauls and the wolf towards the Romans. Livy records that the Gauls killed the deer but the Romans stood back to allow the hunter safe passage with some impromptu seer crying out, *"that way flight and slaughter have shaped their course, where you see the beast lie slain that is sacred to Diana; on this side the wolf of Mars, unhurt and sound, has reminded us of the Martian race and of our Founder"*. Needless to say, the Romans won that particular skirmish.

The Roman writer Petronius produced the torrid Satyricon around the year 61 or 62CE during the reign of Nero. One of the stories contained within it is told by the former slave Niceros, in which he recounts an adventure many years earlier. One night he encouraged an unnamed burly soldier, friend to his owner who was out of town, to join him on a visit to Melissa his mistress (whose husband owned a pub). On the way they stopped off in a graveyard for a rest and the soldier went to relieve himself amid the tombstones (if not a sacrilegious thing to do, certainly an anti-social one). Shortly afterwards Niceros spotted his traveling companion buck naked and stood on the pile of clothing. As the slack-jawed slave watched, the warrior proceeded to urinate whilst turning in a ring to create a circle of pee. Bladder emptied, the soldier transformed into a wolf and ran off leaving his clothes somehow turned to stone. Poor Niceros, scared witless, legged it to his mistress's house only to discover that the wolf had got there ahead of him (no great surprise given how fast they run). The tale says that blood was shed but does not go into detail as to whether there were deaths or injuries alone. Another slave managed to spear this wolf in the neck and drove it off. Niceros returned to his owner's house and there found the soldier bed-bound and under the care of a medicus for a severe wound in his throat. Petronius used the Latin word versipellis, meaning a pelt-changer

It is a common theme in many stories from around the world that shapeshifters who suffer an injury in animal form carry it over when they revert to human guise. Such wounds are often held up as proof positive of the shifter's identity. This particular account is also one of the earliest mentions of someone creating a circle as part of a magical ritual (albeit composed of urine). Doubtless this is part of the bawdy humour in the Satyricon, but it is also likely an allusion to the way wolves mark their territory with pee. Once the clothes are encircled by bodily fluids, they become rock and so cannot be stolen, awaiting the werewolf's return. Part of the psychology of wolves is the potent urge to define and defend their turf, which is something to think about when people engage with lupine spirits in ritual, meditation and so forth. They may well find their own tendency to territorialism increases, which may sit a little awkwardly with some people now that increasing numbers are looking with disfavour on borders and barriers. This is not, say, that practitioners of wolf rituals will suddenly become passionate supporters of political borders, but they may well find themselves growing acutely conscious of personal space and any threat of intrusion upon their turf. In modern national iconography the emblematic animal for Italy is the wolf, Mater Lupa still guarding her borders all these centuries later.

Jumping forward a considerable period of time in Italian history, St Francis was born around 1181 in Assisi. The patron saint of animals and ecology in general and author of the evocative Canticle of the Sun had an encounter with a wolf.

The *Little Flowers of St Francis,* which dates from around 1390, describes how a sizeable wolf was terrorising people in the Umbrian city of Gubbio. The holy man went up into the wilderness outside the city and tracked down the animal. Far from killing it, he made the sign of the cross and converted the beast into Brother Wolf. The two entered the city and Francis brokered a pact in which the citizens would willingly feed their new Brother and he would refrain from scoffing them or their livestock. It is unclear if people in centuries long past genuinely believed animals could embrace Christ, but it is worth remembering that communities around Europe persisted in subjecting assorted animals to court trials for causing deaths, being in league with the Devil, and various other crimes. A fair number of people must have thought that animals could have moral culpability for their deeds.

Chapter 3

On the Wolf Mountain

One of the more gruesome stories told in Ancient Greece was that about the churlish king of Arcadia. The very word Arcadia conjures up images of pastoral bliss, frolicking shepherds and shepherdesses. This owes more to the efforts of the Arcadian Tourist Board than to the actual landscape which is largely mountainous. Slightly differing versions of the story of King Lycaon of Arcadia exist. The common features of the varying accounts suggest that the monarch had fifty sons and that either he, or one of his sons, or the populace of the region wished to test the limits of Zeus's divine powers. The ruler of Olympus descended to the Arcadian mountains disguised as a wandering mortal. He attended a feast thrown by the king where human flesh was served alongside the usual farm animals. Versions differ as to who was chopped up and cooked. Alternate accounts suggests that it was a small child, or a nameless prisoner, and a third version has it that it was one of the fifty princes – Nyctimus. When Zeus realised what had happened, he flew into a divine rage and punished the wicked King before restoring the slaughtered victim to life.

The story offers an interesting theological insight into polytheism, where even the leader of the Olympians is not omniscient and must find things out for himself. The punishment visited on Lycaon and forty-nine of his sons is to be transformed into wolves. It is not explicit if these are ordinary wolves or if they become some variety of werewolf, fusing human intelligence with lupine biology. This myth draws a link between the consumption of human flesh and lycanthropy. It cannot be called cannibalism per se, because Zeus is not eating his own kind, but the implication hovers that an act of human sacrifice also involves the consumption of the dead, whether by the Gods in an abstract sense of by the worshippers in actuality.

The story can be understood as detailing a cultural shift between a period where the early Arcadians engaged in human sacrifice and a time when they gave it up, whether in response to some disapproving sign from Zeus or due to social forces (maybe pressure from neighbouring Greeks who had long since made the change themselves).

Zeus was worshipped in Arcadia under the epithet Lykaios, Wolfish Zeus, where offerings were to him and indirectly to the local lupines to keep them from predating upon the livestock. One of the rituals held in his name was the Lykaia which served at least partially as a rite of passage for pubescent boys. Cook (1914) places this ritual in early May. The exact details of what happened during the rituals are unknown, though the imagery of werewolf transformation – bodies sprouting hair, bones shifting and altering structure, raging hormones etc. have a very obvious link to pubertal changes. The lads may have become as wolves for their entry into adulthood. The Romans believed that much of their culture had been brought to them by an Arcadian, Evander, who arrived some decades before the Trojan War bringing the festival of Lupercalia along with much else.

In his *Republic*, Plato describes a ritual held on the Wolf Mountain once every nine years, in which participants joined a feast which contained a chunk of human flesh. Whoever unwittingly swallowed it would turn into a wolf and remained in that guise until the next gathering. Only if he (or possibly she) had managed to avoid supping on human flesh during his lupine phase would he be able to reassume bipedal form. The nine years may be an arbitrary number, or it may echo the lunations of a human pregnancy with the implication that the wolf-phase is much like gestation before the emergence of the reborn initiate. The letter theta – Θ – is used to symbolise the ninth digit and in the Greek number-based magical system of isopsephy it represents death – partly perhaps because it is the initial letter of Thanatos, the Greek daimon (spirit) of death. This may seem in direct contradiction to the association with gestation, but it could be taken that the nine hairy years are ones in which the individual has died to humanity and become something most definitely Other. The ceremony held at the end of this duration is a chance for him to die as a wolf and be reborn a Man. In Greek astrological symbolism the letter theta represents the element of earth – wherein the dead are buried, of course. The journey into wolf-form could be taken as a journey into the underworld, into the grave.

Most of these stories have the air of third-hand accounts rather than direct insight and it is quite possible that accounts of differing ceremonies may have been conflated into a general sense that the people of Acadia were very odd and engaged in atavistic rituals. For the storytelling audiences of Ancient Athens, these accounts might have served a similar function to that of the "Wrong Turn" film series for urbanite American cinema-goers in recent times.

Wolves will scavenge carcasses, but substantiating claims that they have an appetite for living human flesh is difficult. Ancient accounts often talk of wolves haunting abandoned battlefields in search of an easy meal. Recorded attacks on living humans are very rare. Whether after battles or some other situation, people may have witnessed the animals running off with an arm or a leg and developed a connection between the idea of wolves and the consumption of humanity.

Records of cannibalism for purposes of survival, as part of ceremonial or magical acts, or simply for culinary pleasure are manifold. The individual willing to bump off a fellow human for a tasty snack must seem like a terrifying predator to the unfortunate dish of the day. All the more so where it is not an isolated murderer but a group that coordinate their attacks much like a wolf pack taking down prey.

Herodotus claimed to have heard of the Neuri tribe (situated somewhere around modern Poland or Belarus) who all became wolves for a few days a year. It is possible that he misunderstood an account of an annual festivity in which the tribe honoured a wolf deity by dressing in furs, or running wild in the woods, or entering trance states. Wolves are certainly a significant feature of Baltic mythology.

Along with the devotional site of Zeus, Mount Lykaion also served as home to shrines of Pan and Apollo, both of whom were understood to have lupine attributes. The latter fathered a son, usually called Miletus though some myths give alternative names, by the Cretan princess Acacallis. Dreading how King Midas would react to this seemingly illegitimate child, the mother abandoned the baby. Apollo reacted by sending his loyal wolves to suckle to infant until such time as shepherds adopted him – a trope already seen in the previous chapter and to be found in many cultures. Miletus grew to become a strapping lad who attracted the unwittingly incestuous lusts of his own grandfather. Understandably wanting to dodge the wandering royal hands, the young man set off for pastures new and eventually founded the Anatolian city names after him (in what is now modern Turkey). As with the tale of Romulus and Remus, the foster-child of wolves goes on to create a notable city.

Apollo's lupine connection also impacted on topography in a story recorded by Pausanias. The writer tells us that Apollo sent his wolves to lead people who lived at the base of Mount Parnassus to the top of the mountain, so that they could escape encroaching floods. The community that they formed in the heights was named Lykoreia, the Wolf City.

Aelian's account suggests that the link between Apollo and wolves goes back to his birth when his mother Leto shapeshifted into a wolf prior to the arrival of the Divine Twins, mainly to avoid detection by a wrathful Hera. Menecrates has it that shortly after the births, a pack of wolves led Leto to the sacred River Xanthos where she could cleanse herself and the neonates with the magical waters. The land through which the holy river flowed was afterwards called Lycia (Wolf Land), now part of Turkey. A temple complex dedicated to the mother and her two children was found about two miles from the remains of city of Xanthos. Both the founding of Lykoreia and the arrival at the river involve wolves as guides, a concept which also appears in Egyptian myths.

Modern Greek folklore incudes stories of the *vrykolakas*, a monster that combines elements of both werewolf and vampire. Written accounts only date back to the 17th century, but oral traditions may, of course, go back further. The word stems from Bulgarian roots, combining words for wolf and hairy. While in most respects a werewolf, the *vrykolakas* story has become fused with elements of vampirism. This is particularly in the manner by which people transform into the monster after death, rising from the grave to predate on the living. There are localised variations in the stories, but common ones involve the spread of disease and a penchant for devouring internal organs (often the liver).

Chapter 4

Herding the Wolves

The Slavic and Baltic countries have an abundance of fascinating mythology, including variant stories involving either a lame wolf or a mysterious man who acts wolf-herder. Sometimes this herder is presented as a wizard-like figure, sometimes as a Christian saint, and sometimes as a fairly obvious euhemerised pagan deity. Saints such as Nikolaus, Martin and George are portrayed in various folklores as having powers to charm or lead lupines. The German folklorist Lutz Röhrich (1956) argued in favour of these saintly herdsmen having their roots in paganism. Another example of a saint who might well blend pagan elements into his story is Sava who purportedly received divine guidance to lead the wolves. Sava had been Serbian royalty before becoming a monk and eventually an archbishop. He is now considered a national patron. The wolf itself is the national animal of Serbia, which may stem from the poetic analogy of the Serbian peoples being the wolves which Saint Sava was called to lead.

Speaking of national imagery, the wolf is also the emblem of Portugal and Turkey (as well as Italy, as mentioned in a previous chapter). A rather torrid Turkish myth describes a military attack on a village which wipes out everyone except for a small boy. He is rescued by a she-wolf, Asena, who suckles him in her cave. As he grows up, he fathers children with his rescuer. She comes to settle in a cave near the Qocho Mountains and gives birth to ten strange beings who are half-wolf and half-human. A similar case of cross-breeding takes place in an Inuit story recorded by Franz Boas in 1889. In that account the maiden Niviarsiang marries a dog called Ijirqang and having ten offspring. Half of these are normal puppies, whilst the other

27

five are creatures called adlet. These large beings somewhat resemble centaurs inasmuch as their lower halves are canine and the upper halves human. The puppies become the ancestors of Europeans (at least in the Victorian-era version, other variants may have existed in earlier centuries before contact was made) whilst the adlet sired various groups on the North American continent. Returning to the Turkish account, one of the wolf-men born in the mountain cave was named Yizhi Nishidu, and eventually led the pack of wolf-men who became ancestors of the Ashina clan that dominated the Turkish nomads and took their name from the great she-wolf.

The story clearly has considerable resonance with the Roman foundation story of Lupa and the twins Romulus and Remus. The Chechen culture hero Turpalo-Noxchuo was also believed to have been reared by wolves, leading to the prevalence of lupine imagery in Chechnya. Whilst a great geographic gulf exists between Turkey and lands of the Inuit, it is of definite note that both should have foundational myths in which human civilisations are descended from interspecies relationships between humans and canines or lupines.

Putting aside nauseating genres of pornography, the notion of human-wolf (or any other animal) sexual contact could potentially be interpreted as accounts of tribal exogamy. Quite a number of tribal cultures give themselves titles that essentially translate as 'the People' or a similar concept with terms used to describe all other ethnic groupings as less than human. The representation of tribal groupings by what might loosely be called totemic imagery (though that word should not really be used in quite so free a manner as some more New Age books tend to) is quite common in many societies. Communities might refer to themselves as the People of the Horse, the Bear, or the Oak Tree etc. Such emblems are utilised in a variety of ways, but a not uncommon one is to regulate marriage. In one part of the world the People of the Crow might be obliged to only marry someone from the Salmon Clan or the Owl Clan. In a different culture sexual relationships between the Badger Clan and the People of the Yew Tree might be considered tantamount to incest. In this context, tales such as the Turkish and the Inuit one might stem from a period in which a Clan with whatever totem broke with tradition (perhaps following a major drop in population, whether due to warfare, plague or anything else) and married into the People of the Wolf. The notion that the results of such a union might be bizarre monsters could reflect deeply ingrained anxieties around inbreeding with taboo groups.

Renowned Serbian philosopher and classicist Veselin Čajkanović (1924) preserved a great deal of Slavic mythology and folklore including stories of the various wolf-herders. He was fascinated by the seemingly lost world of Serbian paganism and sought to reconstruct what he could of it, much to the disgust of the rabidly atheist Communist regime. Slovenian ethnographer Mirjam Mencej (2001) proposes that the wolfherders carry out three primary functions: not only do they lead the animals from place to place, but they also feed them (sometimes this is a case of bringing the wolves to the offerings left out for them by humans), and finally protecting humans and their livestock from the hunger of the wolves. In protecting people from wolves, it also has to be said that their herders shield the wolves from the violent vengeance of humans. An earlier chapter discussed the Graeco-Roman festival of Lupercalia, the character of which had been half-forgotten even in the ancient world. it may well be that the early version of Lupercalia involved requests to a herder-like figure to steer the wolves away from the realms of husbandry and into more distant climes where they could not threaten human interests. The herders are a reminder of an era which the Norwegian environmental campaigner Arne Naess would have approved of, where those animals against which humans compete for resources were accommodated rather than eradicated.

Mencej notes that Slavic folk calendars also have festivities centred around wolves, often mediated through the lens of the wolf-herding saint rather than directly on the animals themselves. These tend to fall at either the beginning or end of the herding seasons for sheep or other livestock. At the start of the season pastoral people might well seek divine intercession to protect their animals, whilst at the end of the season the focus would be more of a thanksgiving for however many sheep survived without being carried off by wolves. She lists a variety of ritualistic acts intended to have an apotropaic effect that were carried out on these saints' days.

One category of spiritual being much featured in mythology of the area is a forest-dwelling entity known by a wide variety of names in the regional languages and dialects of Central, Eastern and South-eastern Europe (so many names that one might wonder if they are actually a number of different rather than variations of the same creature). The names Mežainis, Miško velnias, Gayevoi, and Borovoi emphasise the link to forests where the entity (or race of entities) is often visualised in much the same way as Tolkien conceived of the ents – moss-covered guardians of trees and forest animals, practically walking trees themselves. The lupine connection is more to the fore when these beings, if they are the same thing, are called Lesovik, Leshy, Lesun and Lesnik. The Lesovik is often depicted as a rather dishevelled old man with twigs and leaves in his hair, able to summons and lead the wolves whether with a musical instrument (a little like the Pied Piper) or the power of his own voice. It is a wonderfully evocative image that stirs the soul, it is also essentially the same image attributed to the Estonian old man of the forest, Metsavana. Whilst the Lesovik, Lesun etc. is largely assumed to be some kind of fairy or supernatural being, it is worth considering that many people the world over have claimed to have mysterious powers over particular types of creatures – horse whisperers, crowmen, snake charmers etc. That some people should assert powers over wolves is not unexpected, nor is the likelihood that such people should be rather feared and perhaps live on the outskirts of polite society as a result.

Čajkanović argued that one of the ancient deities was at the root of the wolf-herder, such that he was essentially a singular god known by many names rather than a race of supernatural beings. A strong candidate for this euhemerised deity is the Slavic god Veles. He is the patron of livestock, wild animals, music, and the realm of the dead, looking after the recently departed much as he does the wolf packs and the bears of the wilderness with whom he also has a special connection.

In Slavic myth Veles offends the thunder deity Perun by stealing his cattle (in some variations he abducts a family member). This fits well with his patronage of predatory animals like the wolf which is seldom beloved by any farmer whose livestock has been carried off. After Serbia converted to Christianity in the 9th century, such few literary sources as mentioned Veles did so in the context of a frightening, satanic figure. Whether the ancient polytheists saw him in so menacing a role is a difficult question to answer with any certainty.

The god Dažbog sometime takes the form of a white wolf that walks with a limp. He is a patron of miners, wealth, and generosity. The lameness is retained when he is described in human form, often as an elderly man wearing pelts. He is regarded as an ancestral figure of the Serbs, which may well be why the wolf remains the national animal of Serbia. With the conversion to Christianity, Dažbog came to be seen as increasingly akin to Satan if not actually him in another guise. Some European folk traditions claim that Lucifer or the Devil became lame after being expelled from Heaven and falling all the way to the infernal realms. The 18th century French novelist Alain-René Lesage described Asmodeus as having a bad limp resulting from a battle with a fellow demon.

There are non-demonic mythological beings who are also portrayed as lame, most obviously some associated with blacksmithing such as the Greek god Hephaestus, the Roman Vulcan, and the Saxon Wayland Smith. Whilst the latter figure was intentionally hobbled to stop him taking his skills elsewhere, there is the likelihood that the use of arsenic in early smithing may well have led to a range of medical problems one of which is lameness.

One poetic work, the late 12th century *Tale of Igor's Campaign*, includes the story of Prince Vseslav who became a wolf by night and on one occasion travelled from Kiev to Tmutorokan – a journey of roughly 740 miles in a night! This could be discounted as storyteller's licence, or it might be potentially an allusion to someone travelling in astral form. Possibly Vseslav was adept at some shamanic-style skills such as projecting himself psychically in animal guise. Some of the European werewolf trials involved claims that people could move at immense speed once turned into wolves.

The Lithuanian capital city of Vilnius was traditionally founded with the aid of a wolf. The *Geležinis Vilkas* or Iron Wolf is mentioned in the Lithuanian Chronicles which date bck to the 1400s. The tale runs that Grand Duke Gediminas awoke from a nap after hunting an aurochs near the Valley of Šventaragis and reported to his pagan priest Lizdeika that he had dreamt of a huge iron wolf standing on a hill and howling at tremendous volume. The priest regarded this dream as a great omen or both duke and country alike. Gediminas inaugurated the building of what would eventually become the city of Vilnius on that very spot. A number of cultures, some already mentioned, regard themselves as having been descended from wolves. This story gives a variation on that with the city rather than the people owing its existence to a lupine patron.

Another Lithuanian tradition finds echoes in Germanic ones too. The *laukų dvasios* are the spirits of the fields, whose presence is noted when strange movements occur in the crops. The exact movement links the spirit to the animal form it is taking, one of which is the *vilkas* or wolf-shaped spirit. German folklore speaks of the *kornwolf*, a green-furred lupine who makes the crops rustle and move oddly as it goes about bringing a good harvest. Depending on the type of crop they are also called *roggenwolf* (rye wolf), *getreidewolf* (grain wolf), or even *kartoffelwolf* (potato wolf). The generic name for these German spirits is *feldgeister*. Both the Lithuanian and German entities can influence the weather as well as plant growth. It is a common practice to dedicate the last sheaf of corn, or other type of crop, from the harvest – sometimes just left in a corner of the field and sometimes made into a corn dolly or similar ornamental image.

Romanian mythology is heavily influenced by the ancient Dacian culture that went before it. The primary deity Zamolxis transformed one of his priests into an enormous white wolf that could defend the Dacians from the Roman invaders. The Dacian draco was a wind instrument carried into battle, somewhat like a carnyx in design with one end shaped as a wolf's head, though the word draco means dragon. The noise caused by blowing on it can only be imagined. Ovid described the Dacian warriors as *"crueller than wolves"*. Mădălina Strechie (2014) suggests the very name Dacian stems from a root meaning those like wolves. The herder of wolves can be considered as much guardian of the Wolf Tribes as of the animals themselves.

Chapter 5

A Wolf Age

The most famous wolf of Norse myth is, of course, Fenrir. The offspring of Loki and the giantess Angerboda, he takes his name from the dank, mist-shrouded fenlands in which he dwells. He went on to father two wolves of his own, Skoll and Hati, who chase the sun and moon across the sky. Come the battle of Ragnarok his two children will succeed in devouring the celestial bodies (which might be taken to represent eclipses of sun and moon) whilst Fenrir himself will kill Odin. Fenrir will, in his turn, fall to Viðarr who avenges his father Odin and becomes one of the few deities to survive Ragnarok. Both these events are predicted in the poem *Völuspá* where the prophecy is made by a volva. The battle between Viðarr and Fenrir is carved into the Gosforth Cross in Cumbria, which dates to the 900s.

Fenrir was not born a world-devouring monster. The mechanics by which a giantess and an Aesir can become parents to a wolf cub (or a sea serpent, for that matter) are rather glossed over in myth, which is possibly just as well. Having been born, Fenrir grows at a phenomenal rate and presumably eats at a comparable measure too, fed by Tyr. This is alarming enough in itself, but coupled with a prophecy that the cub will grow to wreak havoc, the gods panic and decide to take measures before it is too late. An assortment of evermore magical chains were wrapped around the young lupine, which he shrugged off as part of an apparent game of strength. Eventually the Aesir commissioned the most mystical chain imaginable, named Gleipnir. Made by the dwarves, the chain was composed of the beard of a woman, the breath of a fish, the footfall of a cat, the sinews of a bear, the roots of a mountain, and the spittle of a bird. Being an object of wonder, the chain was exceedingly thin

– so much so that the wolf became deeply suspicious that some trickery was being played on him. Fenrir refused to be bound with Gleipnir unless one of the Aesir put a hand in his mouth as a display of trust. As told in the *Gylfaginning*, the only deity willing to chance this was the warrior Tyr, who lost that hand as soon as Fenrir realised that the seemingly fragile chain would keep him immobile for an eternity.

The Aesir had brought the mighty wolf to an island in Lake Amsvartnir in order to chain him up and there he remains, the chains binding him to massive stones. The island of Lyngvi was held so sacred that the gods would not defile it by shedding Fenrir's blood. Realising the extent of the trick that had been played upon him, Fenrir attempted to bite his captors. The Aesir responded by jamming a sword into his open jaws, preventing him from ever closing his mouth again. The slobber that runs from his open maw forms the River Ván. Curiously the name of the river translates as hope – perhaps indicative that as long as the river continues to flow it is a hopeful sign for the world. The day the Ván ceases will be the day that the wolf is free and wreaking a world-shaking revenge. A somewhat pessimistic view, but perhaps in keeping with the general worldview.

The *Gylfaginning* predicts all manner of devastations caused by Fenrir. In some sense Fenrir is a physical embodiment of Ragnarok itself, the looming doom of the world. Pluskowski (2004) coins the pithy term *lupine apocalypse* to describe the way the giant wolf stands athwart the Heathen and Christian views of a hellish maw that will gobble up the world. Langer (2018) ties the fears of the world ending to a variety of astronomical events that could have been readily witnessed during the ninth and tenth centuries ad regarded as ill omens. He conjectures that the 12th century manuscript '*De ordine ac positone stellarum in signis*' refers to the constellation of the Hyades by the purportedly pre-Christian name of Ulf's Keptr, the wolf's jaw.

This particular star pattern forms the backdrop to some of the gloomy meteorological events that Langer outlines.

Just as many people became anxious in the lead-up to the second millennium so earlier generations worried about the first one. The worries may have persisted long after the turn of the year 1000, having become a substantial part of literary tradition and folk beliefs by the time the *Gylfaginning* was *being* written in the early 1200s.

Having fed the cub all his life, Tyr ends up feeding his own flesh to the wolf. As his sole feeder, Tyr becomes something akin to a foster-father. The wolf's actual father, Loki, also ends up bound to a rock, with entrails rather than chains, and only released at Ragnarok.

A somewhat heated debate continues within modern Heathen circles as to whether Ragnarok is indeed part of ancient polytheist tradition or if it was a concept artificially introduced only in the Christian period to align with the Biblical Armageddon. The penultimate verse of the Hákonarmál speaks of Fenrir being unleashed to cause mayhem. It was composed in honour of the Norwegian King Hakon, who died in 961, by his royal skald. Norway was slowly becoming Christian at this period, so the verse is not conclusive proof one way or the other about the theological origins of Ragnarok. At least some Heathens regard the prophesised end of the world as part of ancient eschatology. It is preceded by a three-year long unrelenting winter, the Fimbulwinter, which might well have inspired part of the Narnia story. To some this is prescient of a nuclear winter and the spectre of a war that really will end all wars. The nuclear winter is a hypothetical scenario, coined by Turco in 1983, who estimated that it would last anything up to four years. Gundarsson (1993) considers the story to be more emblematic of the soul's journey towards growth and the various deaths and rebirths it must undergo, rather than a tale of the whole world ending.

The reader might regard Fenrir as an actual entity, a being of vast power that could easily cause untold destruction if unrestrained. Some readers might see Fenrir as more symbolic than actual, representative of the entropy that exists within all things and will ultimately consume them when the time comes. The release of the Fen Dweller is referred to as the Wolf Age, Vargöld, a poetic kenning for a generally awful time when chaos and suffering reigns.

Odin is served by two rather more benevolent wolves, Freki and Geri – the Ravenous One and the Greedy One. The old adage about wolfing food dates back a long way. The *Gylfaginning* suggests that Odin subsists on wine alone and passes the food from his banqueting table to the two wolves. A straightforward interpretation would be that Odin does not partake of the ethereal food of the Aesir. Alternately it might be considered that any food offerings made by mortals to Odin are consumed by Freki and Geri rather than by the Allfather. In an era when a great many culinary sacrifices were being made, the wolves would indeed need to be ravenous and greedy to devour them all. It may be that ritual offerings were placed in locations where wild animals might eat them on behalf of certain deities. Speidel (2004) suggests that the two figures can also be thought of as sacred warriors dressed in wolfskins, members of the *Úlfhéðnar* – the bands of warriors who donned pelts and entered into frenzied trance states prior to going to battle. Possibly it was they who received food offerings on behalf of Odin, in a manner somewhat reminiscent of the priests of Offler devouring the sausages served up to him. The interpretations of wolves or men are not mutually exclusive. A variety of historians, mythographers and others have considered the wolf-warrior bands to be the practical root of werewolf stories – it is certainly easy to imagine terrified villagers glimpsing pelt-covered men howling and cavorting in the dark woods, visiting violence on enemy tribes.

In a singularly horrific scene one of Loki's sons, Vali, is forcibly turned into a wolf by the Aesir and set upon his own brother, Nari. The disembowelled corpse of Nari becomes the source of the entrails used to bind Loki to a rock as a punishment for his part in the death of Baldr. The lupine Vali reinforces the association between wolves and violent death.

In one of his schemes, Loki brings about the death of the beautiful Baldr despite his mother's efforts to make him invulnerable to all harm. The deities intend to cremate Baldr aboard his own ship, Hringhorni, but it becomes stuck in a sandbank. Not even Thor is able to shift it and they have to send for the strongest being in the Nine Worlds, the giantess Hyrokkin. The *Gylfaginning* describes how she arrives riding on the back of an equally massive wolf which has to be pinned to the ground by four berserkers whilst the giantess moves the ship. She causes an earth tremor in the process. The Valkyrie Gunnr also rides a wolf, lending her name to the kenning Gunnr's mount as a poetic allusion to a wolf. Later folklore from Scandinavian countries includes witches and other dangerous magical figures riding about on normal sized wolves.

Another jotun or giant with lupine connections is Eggþér. His name means Edge-Servant and he acts as a shepherd for the giantesses. When not guiding the livestock, he rears massive wolves or more properly *vargr*, quite possibly including the one ridden by Hyrokkin. One of his functions might have been to rally his wolves ready to go into battle against the Aesir and anyone else the giants chose to war against. These *vargr* went on to inspire the slavering wargs which Tolkien worked into his Middle Earth saga.

Whilst it is only an unsubstantiated personal gnosis of this author, the wintery god Ullr has always appeared in dreams etc. accompanied by a wolf. Ullr, who is also closely associated with archery as well as skiing, skating, and other winter sports, is described as living in Ydalir the Yew Dale. This is fitting for a god of the bow, the yew being one of the best woods for making bows. He was considered one of a small number of oath gods, deities who would oversee the swearing of vows and ensure that people lived up to their word. The *Skáldskaparmál* refers to him as a shield-god, a device sometimes referred to by the kenning of Ullr's ship. This is a possible reference to large shields being used rather like sleds during heavy snows.

Residents of East Anglia on the eastern side of England might be interested in the historical background to one of our major archaeological sites, Sutton Hoo. In 1939 archaeologists unearthed a funereal ship buried beneath a mound and filled with fabulous treasures. The ship is believed to be the last resting place of King Raedwald. He was a prominent member of the Wuffinga lineage that traced its roots back to the Swedish monarch Wuffa (Little Wolf). Under Raedwald Suffolk became the seat of Britain's High Kingship. The descendants of Wuffa are essentially the Wolf's People, a fact marked by the inclusion of the fabulously ornate garnet-covered money bag the clasp of which depicted what we can but assume to be Odin flanked by his two wolves, Freki and Geri, whose carnivorous habits have already been discussed earlier in this chapter.

The last British monarch of the Wuffinga line was Edmund whose severed head was guarded by a talking wolf – still to be seen on the crest of Bury St Edmunds in Suffolk. Edmund was born on December 25th 841 CE (birth on Christmas Day was considered a forewarning sign of lycanthropy in many European cultures, though that is unlikely to have any connection to the saint) and took the East Anglian kingship in 856. He was martyred by members of the Great Heathen Army in around 869 or 870, who tied him to a tree and demanded that he renounce his Christianity. This he refused to do and so was subjected to a fusillade of arrows. Quite how anyone knows he was pressured to turn against Christ is unclear, given that the only witnesses to the killing were the people doing it and they left no account of their deeds. To add insult to injury they decapitated the king and threw the head into the woods. Edmunds followers eventually found the body but were unable to locate the rest of their monarch until they heard a voice cry out *"Hic, hic, hic"*, which is Latin for *"here, here, here"*. Tracking the voice they found a highly educated wolf standing guard over the head that once bore a crown. That the final branch of Wuffa's tree should be watched over by a wolf is, of course, deeply symbolic and speaks far more to the Heathen roots than the Christian limb. Edmund was martyred on November 20th, his feast day, and remained the patron saint of England until finally being displaced by George – who has lupine connections of his own in Central and Easter European countries.

After the last Wuffinga shuffled off to his heavenly reward, the local Angles still kept the creature in their hearts. A little-known nobleman called Ulfcytel the Bold (*Wolf's Cauldron* ~ an odd sounding name, but cauldron was used to mean a generous man to whom everyone flocked, like hungry people round a stew pot) came to lead the area as ealdorman. He was so successful that East Anglia became known for a while as Ulfcytel's Land ~ the Land of the Wolf's Cauldron! In 1016 he fought the battle of Seven Hills near Ipswich, before dying in the October of that year at the Battle of Assandun in Essex.

As a final Suffolk aside (if the reader will excuse the author indulging an interest in his home county) the Shotley Peninsula has long been home to the Norman Vise-de-Loup family (whose name, in all the variant spellings that have changed over the centuries means Wolf's Face – their crest being three wolf heads). The Normans were, of course, the North Men in their origins. It is curious that one relatively small region should have so many recurrent lupine connections.

Chapter 6

Ants of Ancient Land

Even into Shakespeare's day Ireland was euphemistically referred to as the Wolf Land, such was the purported abundance of the animals there. A fair number of mythological characters and legendary accounts connect to wolves in some capacity within Irish, Welsh and other Insular Celtic sources. The title of this chapter derives from a rather graphic episode in the rambling tale of Da Derga's Hostel. In ancient Ireland, as in so many collectivist cultures, hospitality towards strangers as well as kith and kin was a highly regarded virtue. As communities grew in size, the capacity to provide hospitality to large parties of visitors became a challenge. Partly as a result of this, the profession of *briugu* or hospitaller emerged in which some ran what were effectively hotels to house, feed and otherwise accommodate guests. The expenses of such places were met by the local community through taxation. The titular chieftain of the story, Da Derga, owns a famed establishment where King Conaire Mór and his retinue take refuge. The hostel is a magical, Otherwordly place with more rooms in it than a Tardis.

The name Da Derga means "Red God" which grants his property almost the flavour of a temple and those sheltered within could be understood as having been granted sanctuary. The hostel is laid siege by the three foster-brothers of Conaire, who have turned against him following his exiling of them for the committing of various heinous crimes. To the minds of the ancient Irish audiences hearing this story, the shattering of the links between foster-kin would have seemed quite dreadful and the violation of a fundamental social bond. It is a tragic tale, though perhaps the sheer scale of carnage and butchery makes it all a little too fantastical and implausible for a 21st century audience.

The wicked foster-brothers (Fer Lí, Fer Gar, and Fer Rogein) make multiple attempts at burning the great hall to the ground. They are described as gathering in dark around the hall with their war bands and go *fáelad* or *faoladh* (a-wolfing, sometimes understood as taking on wolf-shape). They throw back their heads, howling and roaring, clattering sword against shield, quite possibly dressed in wolf-skins and doubtless terrorising the life out of anyone who heard or saw them by moonlight.

In Irish, to go a-wolfing is akin to the Norse notion of going a-viking. Bands of (usually) young unmarried men, often of aristocratic lineage, joined together and lived in the wilderness. The legal status of the *diberga* varied over time – sometimes they were condemned as outlaws and at other stages tolerate as a useful resource, mercenary bands that could be called into the service of mainstream society (quite possibly for a fee). St Brigit is described as using milk to wash away "diabolical signs" from *diberga* who converted to Christianity. Whilst this could be purely metaphorical, it may rather more literally refer to tattoos painted on (rather than indelibly marked on) to the warriors to indicate their membership. Quite which deity or deities the *diberga* would have been devoted to is purely a matter of conjecture. There are Irish deities with lupine connections and it may have been one or more of these, such as the Mórrígan.

At one juncture King Conaire wipes out a huge number of his enemies before succumbing to a magical thirst which drives him to madness. He begs one of his loyal followers, Mac Cécht, to fetch him a drink. An earlier Mac Cécht derived his name from the word for plough, but this one is better understood as "son of power". The journey becomes ludicrously long because the rivers have been magically dried up and it is not until he finally arrives at Uaran Garad (n modern day County

Roscommon). Returning to the king, he arrives just in time to see the beleaguered monarch being beheaded. Dispatching the two villains, he sets up the head and pours the cup of water into the mouth. In a scene reminiscent of the story of Bran the Blessed, the head remains animate long enough to recite a praise poem in gratitude.

Following this, Mac Cécht sets off for revenge on the fleeing armies of the *diberga* and their allies. Whilst he deals with many, he is eventually overwhelmed and lies brutally injured on the field of battle. A passing woman, who may possibly be an entity come to guide his final journey, speaks to him and he asks if an insect is nipping at him. She sees that a wolf is gnawing its way into his side and is now head-deep in the wound. Possibly Mac Cécht should be understood as a giant. She announces that it is an *"ant of ancient land"*, a curious euphemism for a wolf. Mac Cécht promptly kills the wolf. This incident might be a metaphor for the banishing of this particular band of *diberga*, dismissing them all as no more consequential than insects. A few sentences later another hero, Conall Cernach, meets with his father who refers to his pursuers as swift wolves. One version of the story has him die on the battlefield whilst another sees him return to his home.

Alongside words like the already mentioned *fáelad* or *faoladh,* Irish and Scots Gaelic also contain other wonderfully evocative wolf-related words such as *faol-conda* (wolfish), *faol-cu* (a ferocious warrior), *faol-rnum* (slinking about like a wolf), *cuana, conairt* or *cuanairt* (terms for a wolf pack), the deliciously evocative descriptive words *faoltac* (a place full of wolves) and *cuanac* (a place haunted by wolves), *an tioma-taisean* (lycanthropy), *coin-rioct* (a werewolf) and doubtless others missed in this troll through dictionaries. One of the Gaelic months was known as *Faoilleach*, the wolf month (the same meaning being ascribed by the Anglo-Saxons and also the Estonians to the same time of year, called *Wulfmonath* and *Hundikuu* respectively) and corresponding to the mid-January to mid-February period.

A more overt tale is that of the three unnamed daughters of Airitech. These werewolf sisters (whether or not their parents are also lycanthropes is not gone into) emerge every Samhain from a cave in modern County Roscommon and lay waste to the local livestock and anyone foolish enough to get in their way. Assorted people try and fail to deal with them until the musician Cas Corach teamed up with the warrior Cailte to defeat the monsters. Cas Corach played his harp to lull the savage beasts, eventually telling them that the music would sound so much better if they listened through their human ears. Once they had reverted to womanly form, Cailte skewered all three with a single throw of his spear. The cave of Cruachan Ai remains a visitor attraction to this day and so far as this author knows is werewolf-free.

The wolf-women fit within a long tradition of destructive "plagues" that must be resolved by various heroic figures as a demonstration of their bravery, cunning, or resourcefulness. There may be a partial recollection of wolf attacks on livestock, perhaps from a period of famine in which wolves become bolder in their intrusions onto human territory. That the attacks are annual events connected to the festival of the dead may also contain some allusion to ritualistic offerings made to lupine deities. Perhaps, like the offerings given to Crom Cruaich in another story, the demands became too burdensome and led to a revolt against a particular cult.

The 13th century law book *Bretha Crolige*, which dealt with the care of the injured or ill, records female werewolves as being one of the sorts of women who could not claim sick maintenance from tribal funds, but had to be cared for by their own families. This regulation also applied to satirists and women who consorted with the Sidhe. Female lycanthropes were regarded as especially dangerous. However, the same text specifies that such women must be tolerated because *"it is fitting revenge which she performs, and does not injure her honour price on account of it"*. Whether the she-wolves were shape-shifting to avenge injustices against themselves, or if they were socially sanctioned heavies hired to redress injustice to others (using conventional violence or possibly by mystical means) is unclear. It is implied that the mostly male *diberga* had their wolfishness tolerated because they could be called upon to right wrongs done by rival tribes or others difficult to reach by conventional legal recourse. The women may have been no different.

The previously mentioned warrior-poet Cailte recites a poem to St Patrick, which is found in *Acallam ne Senórach* (The Colloquy of the Elders), and is called *Memory of the Past*. Translated by Ann Dooley and Harry Roe (1999), this likely 11th century poem runs as follows:

> *Cold winter, a sharp wind, a fierce red stag rises.*
> *No warmth this night on the mountain. The stag is swift to bell.*

> *The stag of Slieve Aughty takes no rest,*
> *Listening to the music of wolves.*

> *Dark Diarmait and I, and Oscar, keen and light,*
> *Heard their music on a freezing night.*

> *Well sleeps the stag in his lair,*
> *Shielded against the very cold night.*

> *Today I am old, I know but few.*
> *On icy mornings I shook my spear.*

> *I thank the King of Heave above,*
> *That I held a host, though tonight I'm cold.*

The music of wolves might be taken in quite a straightforward manner as howling, but it can also be considered a kenning for the battle songs and chants of the Fianna wolf warriors – and maybe the *diberga* by general extension. The stag of the mountain may be just that or a metaphor for Fionn, leader of the Fianna, one of whose sons was Oisin (Little Deer) and whose grandson is the Oscar (Friend of Deer) mentioned in the verse. This is a poem of mourning for all that has passed, sorrowed after by Cailte himself but also all those fierce men and women of the age that is passing.

The magical power of music to intervene with a werewolf (also a female one) is found in the myth told of Mis and Dubh Ros. The maiden Mis appears partway into the tale of how the King of the World (a possible allusion towards one of the Roman emperors) decides to add Ireland to his territories. The Fianna warrior bands are called upon and eventually defeat this putative monarch. The survivors come ashore at the White Strand to collect their dead, which is where the king's daughter not only finds her own father's corpse but sees all the other battle carnage too. She is described as kissing her dead parent and tasting his blood in the process. It could be the taste of blood, or simply the sheer horror of war, but she descends into madness and runs screaming to the mountains. Once there she lives as a wild creature, turning into a werewolf that not only ravages the local farm animals and passing travellers, but manages to live for many centuries. Numerous people try to stop Mis' predations, but meet a bloody fate until eventually the *fili* (an Irish poet-seer) hikes up the mountain with only his harp and his wits.

Dubh Ros lures the werewolf in through use of music but, rather than kill her, he seduces her in a rather ribald scene. Such are his charms that she gradually loses her lupine features over time and becomes the demure maid again who can return to civilisation as the musician's bride.

This can be understood as a tale of PTSD, much like the madness of Lailoken or Merlin following their seeing the butchery of battle. All these stories involve a retreat to the wilderness and rejection of human society in favour of the company of wild animals. Modern readers might well think in terms of the therapeutic value of social withdrawal and time alone in the wilds, especially for military personnel or civilians devastated by grief and carnage. Becoming *mactire* – a son (or daughter, in this case) of the countryside – is a move towards healing rather than a descent into irretrievable madness. These wild ones are, however, dangerous having abandoned social norms. Eventually they must reintegrate into the tribe. The life of a forest hermit in an era of bears, wolves, wild pigs, and limited medical treatments must have been a harsh and probably short one. Reintegration is not simply an enforcement of social norms but a genuine wish to make someone part of the only community that will preserve their life.

The goddess Mórrígan manifests to the warrior Cú Chulainn, offering him both erotic pleasures and her subsequent aid in his battle against the tribes of Connaught who are seeking to invade his own territories. The warrior, somewhat naively, rejects the goddess and she takes umbrage. Later in the myth she attacks him in a variety of shapeshifting guises. As an eel she wraps herself round his ankles as he stands in a river ford and tries to trip him. When this fails, she becomes a wolf and panics a herd of cows into stampeding across the ford, nearly trampling him to death. She then becomes a heifer which joins the flight of cattle. In the surviving myths, this is the only association between the Mórrígan and wolves, though she is linked to the Cave of Cruachain Ai which is the entry to her Otherworldly domain.

Cú Chulainn himself is linked not to wolves but to domesticated dogs, though there is a clear dualism to be read here between the tame and wild. Called Setanta as a child, he acquires his adult name in consequence of having killed the enormous guard dog which the blacksmith Culan released to protect the territory during a feast. He had mistakenly believed all guests to be present, unaware that the boy Setanta was late to arrive. Setanta kills the dog with his Hurley ball in self-defence, but is nonetheless obliged to serve in the role of a guard dog until a new hound can be found to protect the blacksmith's land. The ferocity of the original dog puts it on a par with a wolf as an image of fear and power. He later receives a *geas* (magical taboo) against eating the flesh of a dog. Needless to say, he is tricked into breaking this prohibition and it proves his downfall.

County Tipperary has an ancient site called the *Fulacht na Mór Ríoghna* (cooking pit of the Mórrígan), which was likely a place for cooking and feasting used on a regular basis by groups outside of settled communities – possibly hunting parties but maybe also groups who either chose to live separately or who were banished from towns and villages. Tradition links this and similar sites to the *diberga* outlaw bands. Whilst the link is somewhat speculative, it may be that the *diberga* groups were as much religious as mercenary in character and devoted themselves to a deity, possibly the Mórrígan as suggested earlier.

Some texts refer to the *dlaoi fulla*, which means a wisp or lock of delusion. In the first sense of being a twist of grass (possibly strands woven together to form a cord of some sort) or a twig that has been enchanted, it was believed to be thrown at a person in order to curse them with madness. The alternate translation regards this as a lock of hair, leading some commentators to speculate that there might have been some distinctive sort of haircut sported by members of the *diberga* to declare their allegiance to strangers. The hair style is also sometimes referred to as *culan* (wolf locks). The druids themselves were purported to also have a style of their own, the tonsure of St John, worn by some monks who resisted the fashions favoured by Rome and instead shaved the hair at the front of their head and let the hair at the back grow long, was believed by some to have been derived from the druids rather than having Christian precedence. It is referred to as the *airbacc giunnae*, which the literate 7th century Bishop Tírechán discusses with reference to two druidic brothers who converted and at least one, Máel, had to shave his pagan hairstyle off to allow for the Christian one to take its place. Venclová (2002) has argued that the carved stone head found at Mšecké Žehrovice in the Czech Republic may well depict a druid with this very tonsure.

The legal term *cu-glas*, usually translated as meaning Grey Wolf or Green Wolf (*glas* is the shifting grey-blue-green colour of the sea or of forest foliage seen from a distance), was applied to people who existed outside of the law – just as the Saxons spoke of criminals on the run as Wolfsheads.

Crossing the sea to Wales, in the myth of the dodgy brothers Gwydion and Gilfaethwy were exiled to the forests and mountains for three years by their irate uncle Math Mathonwy. He used his magical powers to transform them into various animals and also make them change sex on a rotational basis. One of these years was spent as wolves, with the unfortunate siblings being required to enter into an incestuous relationship as part of their punishment. They bear a child who, upon being presented at Math's court is transformed from a wolf cub into the boy Bleiddwn (wolf-man). Sadly the character does not appear again in any other surviving Welsh literature of the period, but he or his two brothers Hyddwn and Hychddwn might have been figures of note in myths that have not survived the passage centuries.

The *Bretha Crolige* mentions the wolfish *diberg* as part of a triad with the satirist and the druid, whose legal status may not exceed that of a *boaire* (a cattle baron who also acted as a sort of magistrate, which is quite a high rank for a supposed outcaste, suggestive that they may have been more swords-for-hire than hunted criminals).

A later story involving wolves comes from Giraldus Cambrensis, the 12ᵗʰ century clergyman who almost became a bishop of Wales. His book *Topographia Hibernia*, first issued in 1188, details his experiences of Ireland – he has few flattering things to say about either the land or the people. One account describes a story given to him by a priest sent on a mission to County Meath. The unnamed priest and his assistant broke their long journey, camping in the woods of Ossory (or Osraighe), a kingdom in Leinster covering the area now known as County Kilkenny and part of County Laois. During the night they were approached by a talking wolf seeking clerical help for his dying wife. The animal explains that he and his wife are under a curse that has transformed them into wolf form for a period of seven years. The curse was laid upon the whole of Clan Allta by the mysterious St Natalis. The cause of the saint's ire has long since been forgotten, but the magical effect of it rotates around all Clan members affecting two at a time. The she-wolf has been fatally injured by an arrow and needs the Last Rites to be performed.

The frightened priest follows the wolf to his home and, after some misgivings, eventually provides the necessary sacraments. The wolves are able to partially peel away pelt in order to reveal the human beneath the fur. Quite who the Clan Allta actually are, assuming they are not a literary invention, remains uncertain though the implication is that they were long term residents of that area. The Osraighe tribe take their name from the word for deer, itself suggestive that a tribe linked to the predator lived alongside one linked to the prey. A similar duality is found with the Fianna, whose leading lights have links to deer (such as the shapeshifting Siabh and her child Oisin and in turn his son Oscar). The 11ᵗʰ century Fragmentary Annals refer to the people of Ossory as Clann Connla, the first syllable of which may link to one of the words for a dog or a wolf.

Giraldus echoes the views of St Augustine that shapeshifting is a blasphemous and impossible idea. He suggests that it is simply an illusion caused by magic, a sort of high-end conjuring trick. This may be the reason why Giraldus includes a scene in which the fur of the she-wolf is peeled back like a theatrical costume to reveal the human torso beneath. There is a slim possibility that this may alternatively be a garbled understanding of the kind of shamanic ceremony where magical practitioners dress in animal skins, imitate the behaviour and vocalisations in order to take on the spirit of the creature.

The figure of Natalis is most likely the one also known as Saint Naile, a 6th century descendent of Munster royalty who served as an abbot in County Donegal. His feast day is January 27th. Quite why he cursed the people of Clann Allta is unknown, though another tale might be a parallel to this tale and give some hints. The 13th century Norwegian wisdom text *Konungs skuggsjá* (The King's Mirror) discusses the marvels of Ireland at one point, including mention of a story in which St Patrick curses a tribe of hard-line pagans who have been disrupting his preaching by howling like wolves, which shows that the tactics of modern day cancel-culture exponents are nothing new. Patrick's revenge is to turn the howlers into wolves though with an interesting variation that echoes Giraldus' account of the Ossory wolves. According to the author of the Mirror, at least some of these cursed people are only affected by it once every seven winters' when they become wolves with an appetite for human flesh. Possibly they only become a wolf for the duration of the winter months. It is tempting, given such spooky stories set at Samhain as The Adventure of Nera which involves a talking corpse amongst other things, to speculate that maybe the winter's feast of Samhain was the ominous date of this lycanthropic curse falling on the tribe. Others, he says, remain transformed for seven long years (rather than just a winter) but, having completed their lupine duty, they go back to being human and never transform again. The Norwegian text may be partially influenced by Bishop Tírechán's account of St Patrick calling on God to kill the druid Lochlethlanu who has opposed the saint's preaching. Patrick decries the druid for barking at God like a dog.

A similar account of a lycanthropic curse is given of Patrick's vengeance against the Welsh King Vereticus, though Bernhardt-House (2012) is of the view that this story is purely a translation error by Sabine Baring-Gould in his 1865 tome *Book of Werewolves* where he may have misread a Latin account of Patrick turning Cereticus into a fox. Prior to 1865, no version of the curse on Vereticus appears to exist.

The King's Mirror goes on to discuss *gelts*, a term used to describe people experiencing mental collapse. The book describes how the inexperienced who participate in battle sometimes lose their minds and run off into the woods and mountains to live as animalistic hermits. This is essentially what happens in the previously mentioned story of Mis and Dubh Ros and again seems a basic understanding of what we now call PTSD. Where the Norwegian version differs from the Irish is in the assertion that, after twenty years of wild living, the afflicted sprout feathers to keep themselves warm. In the tale of Mis she grows fur rather than feathers. Though the image of a human-like figure covered in feathers brings to mind the story of Nemglan and his bird-men but also the accounts of the feathered cloaks, *tuigen*, worn by some members of the *filid* (poet-seers). It is quite possible that initiatory rituals for becoming a *fili* might have involved spending time apart from human society, immersed in the wilds.

Giraldus presents this story matter-of-factly, presumably finding the notion of transformative curses and taking wolves quite plausible. A great many of the things which are largely regarded as fantastical in the 21st century were taken for granted in earlier periods of history.

The *Cóir Anmann* (Elucidation, or Fitness, of Names) makes mention of Laignech Fáelad who is described as the ancestor of the werewolves of Ossory. The book describes the meaning and origin of various personal names. Other texts refer to him as the brother of Feradach mac Duach, a king of Ossory who died around 581 or 583. This would make him a rough contemporary of Saint Naile, who died in 564 and so might have cursed Fáelad and his descendants. However, the list of Ossory's kings given in the Book of Leinster does include an earlier one called Laignech Fáelad, whether these were two distinct people of the same name or if there has been a conflation between historical figures is unclear. A question arises as to whether Fáelad is a historical person or a euhemerised divine being who was considered not so much the founder as the patron deity of the wolf cult.

The Annals of the Four Masters talks of another member of Ossory royalty with lupine connections – Faelchar ua Maelodra, whose death in battle led to various strange and sinister omens including that of a talking wolf. What the wolf said is not accounted for.

The 11th century Latin poem *De mirabilibus Hibernie* (On the Wonders of Ireland) was penned by Bishop Patricius of Dublin and includes mention of lycanthropy, portraying it not as something acquired through magical curse or infectious bite but rather as an innate condition. The translation is by Elizabeth Boyle (2014).

There are some men of the Irish race,
Who have this wondrous nature from ancestry and birth:
Whensoever they will, they can speedily turn themselves
Into the form of wolves, and rend flesh with wicked teeth:
Often they are seen slaying sheep that moan in pain.

But when men raise the hue and cry,
Or scare them with staves and swords, they take flight [like true
wolves].
But whilst they act thus, they leave their true [i.e. their own] bodies
If any man harm them or any wound pierce their flesh,
The wounds can be seen plainly in their own bodies:
Thus their companions can see the raw flesh in their jaws
Of their true body: and we all wonder at the sight.

The reference to injuries in wolf form being duplicated in human form is reminiscent of similar stories from all over Europe and further afield about witches turning into hares and other animals, whose sleeping human bodies acquire the same injuries as those inflicted on what many in the 21st century might describe as an astral body. This may go some way to explaining the quotidian acceptance of lycanthropy evinced by Gerald of Wales, in that the term conflates a wide variety of phenomena and we need to be clear as to quite what a specific culture meant by it. The Irish of earlier centuries may have conceived shapeshifting as more of a psychic act than the dramatic physical transformations of Hammer Horror movies. The practitioner of this style of shapeshifting might enter a trance state in which they assume an astral presence that either rides the body of an actual wolf or takes on a guise which might be perceptible to some people. The 20th century occultist and author Dion Fortune wrote about a personal experience in her 1930 book *Psychic Self-Defence*. On one occasion she lay in bed fulminating about someone who had deeply hurt her when the image of Fenrir Wolf jumped into her mind and she felt it drawing life force from her to become an actualised entity. She describes not only seeing it but also feeling the weight of the manifestation. This suggests, if the description is given plausibility, physical reality that goes beyond a mere dream-image.

Not wanting it to run amok, even against the object of her contempt, she managed to transform the lupine presence into a harmless canine one which gambolled off towards the northern corner of her bedroom and disappeared. She was later able to reabsorb the energy that created this form by addressing the thirst for revenge that had fuelled it.

Fortune described this incident as having happened by fluke when she was young rather than being the intentional magic of the mature practitioner. Imagine such a skill in the hands of someone who knows exactly what they are doing and follows through, their body seemingly asleep whilst fuelling the existence of a wolf-form (the meaning of the surname Fáelad) solid enough to have material weight runs forth. A whole cult of people who could do this would be a force to be reckoned with.

The early Irish alphabet, the ogam, is described in the *In Lebor Ogaim* from 1390 and some other manuscripts. Each letter is described in a number of ways, including some short cryptic remarks referred to collectively as the *Briatharogaim*. One letter, *Huathe*, which is sometimes translated as meaning a hawthorn tree but more properly means fear or terror, is given the following description: *condál cúan* (assembly of packs of hounds or wolves). The connection between the wolf packs, fear, and hawthorn trees is open to debate but the author's suggestion is offered here. The howling of wolves at night may be beautiful to many but can also be frightening, especially to ancient farmers worried their livestock or even that their children might be carried off. As previously indicated, the *diberga* howled as a form of psychological warfare intended to reduce their opponents to gibbering wrecks. One of the reasons why wolves howl is to demark their territory from other packs. Just like the *diberga*, they seek to scare others – which, if successful, might circumvent any need to actually fight them. In a sense, this is why trees like the hawthorn have sharp spikes; deterring grazing animals with a display of defensiveness is a way of avoiding harm rather than causing it. The highly entertaining 2002 British horror film *Dog Soldiers* includes the Uath family who live in seclusion in a Scottish forest and turn out (spoilers) to be werewolves. Presumably the scriptwriter, Neil Marshall, must know at least something about the ogam connection.

The story of the great chieftain Cormac mac Art described him being taken away as an infant and reared by a she-wolf (indeed, Cormac itself means 'wolf-son'). In adulthood he was accompanied by a loyal pack. His mother Achtan had fallen asleep after fleeing a menacing army, when the wolf snuck off with the child and took him to its cave in Kesh. A huntsman eventually found and returned the infant.

Insular British and Irish saints are often portrayed with wolves: the Irish St. Maedoc of Ferns, who died in AD 626, is held to have shared his food with a starving wolf. Sixth century Saint Columban, yet another Irish-born saint living in the forests, was never molested by wolves and lived amicably among them. Over in Galatia, the obscure, ascetic seventh century Saint Theodore counted wolves and bears as his allies. Like Cormac, the Irish Saint Ailbe was suckled by a she-wolf.

Scotland has the charming tale of the Wulver, man-wolf creatures that lived peacefully off fish and would occasionally share their catches with hungry locals in the Shetland Isles. Brian Smith (2021) rejects this account as the result of an over-imaginative misreading of a Norse word meaning elf or fairy (not wolf) by the folklorist Jessie Saxby (1933) whose writing were the earliest account of the wolf-headed fisherman. The wolf-headed fisherman may owe more to her creativity than to traditional Shetland folklore.

Chapter 7

Strength of the Wolf

The Indian wolf (*Canis lupus pallipes*) is smaller than the European timber wolf and lacks the thick winter pelt. They breed between middle October and December and can be found in surrounding countries. Numerous attacks on humans are recorded, though it is not wholly clear how reliable these claims are or whether it is always definitely wolves rather than other predators.

The Rig Veda, a major Hindu text, gives the story of the sage Ṛijrāśhva who received a visit from a donkey used as a steed by the Ashvins (deities of medicine). In a rather odd turn, the donkey shapeshifts into the form of a wolf and seeks help from the sage who offers up a great flock of sheep to her. Ṛijrāśhva is cursed and sent blind by his father in retribution for this act. The text makes it clear that the father is deeply misguided in taking such action for Ṛijrāśhva is honouring the deities with his actions rather than depriving anyone of their herds (or the sheep of their lives). The wolf prays to the Ashvins, praising his generosity as akin to the acts of a devoted lover, and they cure his blindness. General descriptions of wolves in the Vedas tend to be less than flattering, with such adjectives as wicked, inauspicious, and savage (Griffiths translations). One sutra includes the wolf along with five other animals, each a metaphor for a vice that must be overcome. The wolf represents anger.

The Rig Veda also makes brief mention of the Vrikaah, a warrior tribe who act in wolfish fashion. The root of their name is the Sanskrit *vrka*, an ambiguous word that can be translated as either wolf or plough. There are numerous characters in the Vedas named for the wolf. In Ayurvedic medicine wolf flesh is consider one of the *māṃsavarga (animals with medicinal properties)*. The Parāśarasmåti text recommends that a wolf bite be spiritually cleansed by washing and reciting verses from the Gāyatri aloud.

A story told of Krishna describes his frustration in motivating the citizens of Vraja to move to Vṛindāvana, both of which are in the Uttar Pradesh state. Modern Vṛindāvana has lost much of its former natural beauties to relentless urbanisation – some of which is, ironically, happening to accommodate the vast numbers of pilgrims visiting every year. In order to get the people moving he plucked hairs from his body and transformed them into wolves which harried them in the right direction much like sheepdogs. These were not the first wolves to appear in the world, but just appeared to serve a function. It is not clear what happened to the wolves once the migration was completed. Their descendants may roam Vraja still.

The famed Sikh teacher Guru Nanak went to Lahore where he met Duni Chand, a wealthy man who was mourning the death of his aged father. Part of the ceremonies was Shradh, the ritualistic sharing of food. Chand stated that he had honoured his father's memory by feeding one hundred Brahmans. The Guru was not so impressed by this and informed him that his father had reincarnated in the form of a hungry wolf. This was due to the old man having his appetite stimulated on his death bed by the smell of nearby cooking. His dying wish had been for the meat, and so becoming a wolf was the karmic way to fulfil that urge. The Sikh faith favours an entirely vegetable diet, regarding meat consumption as weighed down by sin. When Chand claps eyes on the wolf, it dies and confirms to him from the spirit that the Guru's explanation of his reincarnation is correct. The connection between the wolf and hunger is once again reinforced. The Hindu Manusmâti law book suggests that people will reincarnate as wolves if they steal deer or elephants.

Nanak also had an encounter with a shapeshifting Jogi. He had attended a religious rally at the same time as a group of Jogis were hosting a rival event. Jealous of the greater numbers crowding round the Guru, the Jogis attempted all manner of mischief to disrupt what was happening including theft of donations. When that failed one turned into a wolf, another a large cobra, and a third conjured up a rain of fire. Nanak was unmoved by all this and calmly recited a Shabad (hymn) that caused the men to see their own wickedness and convert. The wolf here is a bit of a throwaway image, but is clearly regarded as frightening and dangerous.

The Roman historian Cassius Dio mentioned a strange creature, the *corocotta*, which previous writers had also referred to, as having hailed from India. Photius calls the same animal *kynolykos*, the dog-wolf, suggesting it is a hybrid of the two. Exactly what this animal was, assuming it was real and not a traveller's tale, is open to debate. One source suggested the *corocotta* was actually a hyena rather than a wolf, or possibly a hybrid.

Another strange wolf-like creature hails from the Chitral region of Pakistan, the nocturnal *halmasti*. Sometimes cited chasing alongside vehicles driving at night, the *halmasti* is large up to the size of a horse. To add to the risk it poses, the creature is alleged to breathe fire! The *halmasti* has an appetite for children but can be warded off by the presence of iron objects, an aversion it shares with European fairies. Some Muslims from Chitral keep vigil by recently dug graves, reciting verses from the Quran to frighten of the creature from digging up the body and gnawing on the bones. Whilst the fire-breathing may stretch plausibility, there is clearly a pragmatic risk of wolves, wild dogs, and other canids in scenting carrion.

The belief in jinn (root of the English word genie) is widespread throughout the Islamic world. Understanding of jinn mixes scholarship from the Quran, the Hadiths, and localised folklore. One author of medicinal texts, Abu'l-Mundhir Khaleel ibn Ibraaheem Ameen (2005), states that whilst jinn can engage in extensive shapeshifting, they cannot assume the shape of a wolf and are terrified of wolves. Quite why is unclear, but one source praises the wolf for its purity. This view was recorded amongst the Bedouin, but may also be held more widely than that.

Whilst only tangentially Asian, Rudyard Kipling's 1894 *The Jungle Book* is worth mentioning with the pack of wolves that adopt the abandoned baby Mowgli and raise him as a feral child. Kipling spent his early years in India and was very familiar with the cultures and much of its mythological traditions. Mowgli's four-legged kin include his foster-mother Raksha, the pack leader Akela, Father Wolf, and Grey Brother. Kipling would undoubtedly been familiar with the accounts of feral wolf children from India and elsewhere.

For Kipling the wolves are not only Mowgli's family but also teach him the rules of the jungle, which are essentially ethical principles that can also guide the young readers through life. Many of the indigenous cultures of North America and Canada also see wolves as having a teaching, guiding capacity. The title of this chapter comes from Kipling, *"the strength of the Pack is the Wolf, and the strength of the Wolf is the Pack"*.

Chinese folklore contains the popular 15th century story of *Zhōngshān Láng Zhuàn* (The Wolf of Zhongshan) in which a hunted wolf seeks help from Dongguo, an adherent of the philosophies of Mozi travelling through the same forest. The philosopher smuggles the wolf away from the hunting party only to find the ungrateful beast eager to devour him and using his own philosophies to justify his demand. After much dispute, the two agree to put the case before three wise counsellors. One is an old fruit tree which supports the wolf; another is an old water buffalo who says much the same. Both the tree and the buffalo were once loyal providers whose days of fruit and milk are long past. The people they once served are now ready to kill them for firewood and meat, which the subservient pair see as only right and proper.

The third wise counsellor is an aged farmer who tricks the wolf and batters it half to death. A woman reveals that her child has been eaten by the wolf, whereupon Dongguo finishes the creature off.

The wolf is depicted as utterly untrustworthy and manipulative, contrasting with the naïve and gullible Dongguo. The story is also a critique of Mozi's teachings, which were popular in China for some time (though definitely out of favour with the current Chinese Communist Party). Mozi argued that moral duty was owed equally to all without any of the biases and partiality most people demonstrated to their nearest and dearest. Whilst the other popular philosophies of feudal China, Taoism and Confucianism, thoroughly embraced the notion of filial devotion between family members and friendship circles, Mozi distinguished his teachings by rejecting it. The duty to feed the hungry should be met equally and impartially, even to the comedic scenario where the empty belly in question wants to be filled with Dongguo himself. Whilst wolves often have their ravening qualities emphasised in Chinese stories, in this instance the wolf represents any person or creature that seeks to exploit the gullibility of the well-meaning.

The tree and water buffalo serve to demonstrate what the originator of the story clearly felt to be the inherent servility of Mohist doctrine. One of Mozi's key beliefs was that the state came first and foremost, not only above family networks but also the individual. That these supposed sages will die in the process of serving the community is of less importance than that someone (and here the wolf is the rapacious demands of the state) benefits. Mozi's philosophy foreshadowed the extreme Left-wing ideologies of the 20th century which sacrifice the individual for the supposed good of a hypothetical People.

A salutary story is told of a healer, Bian Que, who finds a man three-quarters dead and in need of a heart and lung transplant. He jumps upon a passing wolf and a dog, slicing the heart out of the first and the lungs out of the second, before inserting them in the patient. The man rapidly recovers only to accuse Bian Que of stealing his original organs and dragging him before a magistrate. The court finds in favour of the healer, declaring the patient to have the heart of a wolf and the lungs of a dog (henceforward a euphemism for ingratitude). Feudal China would clearly have benefitted from Good Samaritan laws. It seems a trifle unfair to blame either wolf or dog for the callow attitude of the injured man.

Japan has a wider number of wolf-related myths than China does, though the Japanese grey wolf (*Canis Lupus Hodophylax*) has sadly been extinct since the turn of the 20th century when the Meiji government committed genocide in the name of modernisation. What might have been the very last wolf was sold as a taxidermy specimen to the British Museum by Japanese hunters. The Hokkaido wolf went extinct about twenty years earlier. The Ainu folklorist Yukie Chiri collected much thirteen *yukar* songs traditionally sung by women and published them as *Ainu shin'yōshū* (Ainu Songs of Gods) in 1923. This proved to be her life's work as she died shortly afterwards. One of the songs is that of the Hokkaido Wolf deity, speaking to the audience in his own words. Unfortunately it has not proved possible to include an excerpt from the Wolf God's song here.

The slaughter of wolves was in complete opposition to the previous reverence displayed towards wolves, partly perhaps because they predated upon the animals that often raided the farmers' crops. Horse breeding communities were less enthusiastic about wolves, but hunting them remained surrounded by taboos until the government drive forced a change of minds.

The wolf deity Ooguchi-no-Magami is honoured with a festival in January. At one of shrines he is also honoured with monthly rituals held on the 19th day. An early legend was told of Prince Yamato Takeru who had become lost in the mountain wilderness, led astray by a demon in the guise of a deer, until a white wolf guided him to safety. Afterwards the prince had temples and shrines built to honour the *kami* (spirit) of the wolf. One of these, the Mitsumine Shrine, remains a popular place of pilgrimage even today. Ooguchi-no-Magami cleansed the area of demons, such as the one masquerading in deer-form, and afterwards received regular offerings of meat. The notion of wolves as guides for the lost crops up in quite a few folktales, perhaps emulating the more famous story of Takeru, and has entered into children's literature. *Sebu to Okami no Yakusoku* (A Promise of Sebu and Wolf) by Hiroshi Hirono and Oki Nako (2008) is a modern spin on the tradition, with a spirit wolf rescuing a lost Ainu child.

An earlier chapter explored the Central and Eastern European tales of the Leshey (and the numerous variants thereof). There are tales of these forest guardians and wolf-herders sometimes helping lost humans find their ways home. Gaelic lore has a very similar figure, the Ghillie-Dhu (the Dark Servant), which whilst having no explicit link to wolves does guard the trees and sometimes rescues lost children.

Whilst the Roman Lupercalia festival likely started as a way for shepherds to bribe wolves into leaving their flocks in peace, the ceremonies for Ooguchi-no-Magami seem more an encouragement to chase the deer, wild pigs, and other herbivores away from the rice paddies. The environmental scientist and head of the Japanese Wolf Association, Naoki Maruyama (2014) has noted the increasing problems caused by having burgeoning deer and pig populations devouring plant life without the restraining power of the wolves. Maruyama favours the reintroduction of wolves (albeit to could no longer be the extinct native population) in order to restore nature's balance.

He is credited with evaluating the worthiness of the people that come before him. There is a similar idea to be found amongst the Chukchi people of Russia who believe that two huskies guard the entrance to the Afterlife and only allow those who were kind to dogs to pass on through. Curiously, genetic research reveals that the Chukchi are kin to the Ainu people of the Japanese island of Hokkaido.

The Taoist stellar god Myoken Daibosatsu, who became absorbed into Buddhism as a bodhisattva, sent a white wolf as a messenger to Okubo Samanosuke, an old family retainer who was headed to a shrine to pray for his Master's recovery from illness. He resisted the urge to kill the old wolf he saw sitting under a camphor tree. As a result Myoken guided Okubo to a hot spring which cured numerous ailments. The role of wolf as healer merits greater analysis.

Chapter 8

Opener of the Ways

As outlined in a previous book about Egyptian mythology (*Pantheon – The Egyptians*), there is an ongoing discussion in Egyptology circles around the exact nature of the animal depicted as the head of the deity Wepwawet. Some argue that it is a jackal head, possibly of a different subspecies from the head of Anpu (whom the Greeks called Anubis). Others, this author included, regard it as the head of a wolf. The Ancient Greeks shared the belief that Wepwawet was a wolf and so referred to the deity's chief site of worship as Lycopolis, City of the Wolf.

Modern zoologists have suggested that the creature in question is *canis anthus lupaster*, which has been classified as a wolf by some and a jackal by other researchers. Whilst clearly some will not agree, for the purposes of this chapter Wepwawet will be treated as decidedly lupine. From a theological stance, it is worth noting that a deity will manifest as whatever it pleases to differing peoples so that the lupine perspective is not mutually exclusive to the other canine interpretations.

Whilst family trees in Egyptian mythology vary by region and historical era, Wepwawet is often described as a son of Setekh (whom the Greeks called Set or Seth), and therefore brother to Anpu (Anubis). Along with Anpu he is one of the deities with jurisdiction over the dead.

The name translates as Opener of the Ways (or Roads). As such he may have had duties towards travellers over land and possibly road-builders as well. Other titles attributed to him include Extinguisher of Breaths, emphasising his obligations towards the deceased and maybe even placing him in the role of a Grim Reaper figure charged with cutting the thread of life itself. At risk of romantic whimsy, one could see the wolf's jaws snapping shut upon that delicate cord.

Wepwawet holds a central role in Egyptian mythology, standing at the head of the solar of Re, ready to open the gates as the boat descends into the west at sunset and open the eastern gates as it rises at dawn. Not only does he open the gates but, as a deity with a close relationship with the military, he battles the forces of chaos in the Underworld.

Perhaps this set precedence, because parades involving the Pharaoh would often be led by someone bearing the standard of the wolf. If a rationalisation is required, people might have followed the paw-prints left by wolves in the sand possibly as a way of finding water or dead bodies.

In honour of the military link, Wepwawet carried a mace and bow and arrows. Another of his symbols is the *shedshed*, the exact meaning of which is somewhat mysterious. The depiction of the *shedshed* changes over time, some version showing a simple curved line rather like a sickle blade but later versions becoming very puffed up and looking rather more like a fleshy kidney. Evans (2011) conjectures that the *shedshed* represents the wolf's den, based partly on comparisons to depictions of the burrows and homes of other animals in Egyptian art. Other Egyptologists have suggested different interpretations, such as the puffier shape being a cushion or placenta, but Evans argues these views to be misguided. She highlights a passage from the Pyramid Texts which indicates that the *shedshed* is involved in the dead pharaoh's ascent to the heavenly realms (though quite how is unclear). Evans goes on to explain the connection between the Opener of the Way and the pictogram of a den is that the den here is a dug-out burrow rather than the cave beloved of Roman imagery. The wolf that digs out a den from packed soil is opening a way for himself and his mate, offspring etc. to a place of safety. It could also be interpreted as symbolically digging a grave, though more of the sort used by the financially impoverished Egyptians rather than those of royal blood. In terms of the ascent of a deceased monarch, the *shedshed* could indicate that Wepwawet might have been understood as helping the discarnate soul find its own den or home in the Afterlife by clearing away whatever blockages stand in the way. Those blocks would clearly not be sun-baked soil but perhaps the weight of past sins – too much *isfet*, or chaotic and discordant actions – or the magical efforts of the pharaoh's enemies to disbar him from a paradisiac existence.

If this suggestion about sweeping away barriers in the Afterlife (which is this author's, not Evans') is accurate rather than mere idle speculation, then perhaps the Great Wolf was turned to by some people to help them purify the burdens on their deceased loved ones or even possibly to help those still living to purge the weight upon them. As a bit of literary whimsy, imagine the Dickensian scene between the ghost of Jacob Marley laden down with the chains he forged in life through his *isfet-ic* avarice and callousness and the living Scrooge who could yet be convinced to live according to the harmonious teachings of *ma'at* and give up his own miserly ways. The Ancient Greeks believed in the threat of *miasma*, actions that could stain the soul, and the rituals of *katharmos* need to cleanse oneself. The Shinto religion of Japan teaches that some deeds and substances pollute a person by generating a sort of psychic taint (*kegare*) and that these can be purified (*harae*) through various methods and rituals (*misogi*). It does not stretch the imagination too far to see the Egyptians seeking divine aid in removing the burden of *isfet* from the dead and potentially the living too. The Great Wolf whose ferocity can fight off the monstrous forces that seek to tear Re from his barque each night might be ideally suited to aid lesser beings in the battle against the corrupting powers.

Wepwawet is one of the key figures in the ceremony of the Opening of the Mouth, which was once performed over mummified bodies as a means to grant them speech and other capacities in the afterlife. Bearing in mind that a significant form of Egyptian magic was the *heka* – spoken (or rather sung) magic in which the sacred names of things, the *renu*, are resonated in order to create or transform them for good or ill. Speaking a brand new *ren*, a power seemingly possessed by the deities alone, causes that thing to come into existence. Without wishing to reduce a profound metaphysical concept to the level of psychobabble, every time a child (or, indeed, and adult) learns a new word, learns the name of the thing before them for the first time they internalise it as a mental construct or schema. Putting a name to something creates it within our own psychic space. Almost without exception words are learnt from someone else, so this becomes not only an internalisation of a new idea (words are not just new sounds, but import a whole baggage of notions with them) but also induction into what Edmund Husserl called *Lebenswelt* (Lifeworld). The Lifeworld is a kind of mental Matrix shared by everyone else living and dead who has also understood the same concepts and notions.

It could be debated at some length as to quite what is meant by the Opening of the Mouth and what it implies if the ceremony does not occur. One suggestion, favoured by this author, is that the dead whose mouths remain unopened are the ones that can no longer communicate with the living or pass on their guidance.

One festival associated with the wolf god is the *Heb-Sed*, which happened very rarely indeed as a jubilee marking the thirtieth anniversary of a pharaoh's reign and the subsequently at three- or four-year intervals following that (such festivals must have been very few indeed given the ever-present threats of disease and warfare, though Rameses II was an exception to this with over six decades on the throne).

Vegh (2009) notes that the Procession of Wepwawet occurred in the first month of the Egyptian calendar *Tekh* in the season of *Akhet*. Whilst the exact start of the year is a bit of a moveable feast, the Procession (which likely involved the carrying out of a sacred statue in public) would be roughly late August to September on the modern calendar. The Procession kicked off the *Haker* festival which commemorated the dead during the Middle and New Kingdoms. Anthes (1974) suggests the statue of Asur (called Osiris by the Greeks) was moved from the temple at Abydos to a location by a lake during this event. It may be the product of excess imagination, but it is easy to envision a re-enactment of the daily barque journey in which a statue of Wepwawet stood at the prow of the parade, opening up the way for the statue of Asur to follow. A significant focus of the *Haker* was to provide the pharaoh with an opportunity to reassert his link to the deities, especially Asur as the embodiment of the lineage of all deceased pharaohs whom he would ultimately join.

The Greek-Sicilian historian Diodorus Siculus, claimed that an Egyptian wolf deity called Macedo or Macedon was the brother of Anubis. How accurate Diodorus' understanding of Egyptian culture was is rather open to debate. Macedon is later described as having become king and patronym of the Macedonians, which is not the case. There is a potential explanation for the confusion in that a work by Plutarch refers to Alexander the Great as the arch-wolf of Macedonia, possibly a reference to his cunning or to his predatory appetite for new territories. If this title were also familiar to Diodorus, he might have confused one arch-wolf with another. Diodorus also suggests that Osiris (Asur) returns from the dead in the guise of a wolf – a story which does not appear in the surviving translations of Egyptian myths, but may once have done so – to aid his widow and child who were being menaced by Typhon (the name Diodorus gives to Setekh or Set). The 4th century Greek historian Eusebius echoes this account. Diodorus adds that, following the death of Typhon, Osiris' followers declare that the wolf is his holy animal and should be worshipped as such. He also suggests that a vast band of wolves once drove the Ethiopian armies out of Egypt, an event that again does not appear in any of the translated Kemetic historical documents. This is a little reminiscent of Krishna's wolf army that pushes the people of Vraja on to their new homeland. Another act of benevolence by wolves recorded by the Greek writer Herodotus is that of two lupines aiding a blind priest of Aset (Isis) in the capacity of a guide dog. Herodotus only mentions a return journey to a temple, so this may have been a one-off act rather than a lifetime of service.

A variety of wolf folktales are found across the rest of Africa, rather more than can be touched on in a book this size. It is a topic that deserves a book of its own. As a small sample, one South African tale recounts a cunning jackal feigning death to trick a fisherman out of his catch. The wolf tries to emulate the trick and ends up battered senseless. Quite a few African tales focus on the gormlessness of the wolf rather than its cunning, much as some modern American tales see the creature as the butt of jokes. A West African story depicts a thieving wolf nightly robbing an old lady of her sheep until a lion comes to her aid and pretending to be a sheep in order to kill the wolf. This echoes the widespread agrarian view of wolf as unwanted competitor for food.

Chapter 9

Huff and Puff

Wolves often appear in the folklore and fairy tales of Europe as well as that of other continents. This chapter will explore some of the key tales from Europe, drawing on psychological and sociological explanations of the insights such curious accounts can offer. The notion that such stories cannot be wholly dismissed as merely quaint children's tales is not new.

The American author and therapist Colette Dowling wrote *The Cinderella Complex* (1981) which suggested that storytelling can have a powerful and sometimes negative effect on impressionable young psyches to the extent of pushing girls towards a passive, dependent approach to life in which they wait for Prince Charming to come along and sort out their miseries. Simply reading or hearing a story once will not cause psychological harm, but Dowling's contention was that certain stories saturate cultures and are heard so often that the constant exposure does indeed have a cumulative impact.

The sociologist Jim Sidanius outlined the potency of what he referred to as legitimising myths, widely held stories told within a culture that promote a way of life as normal and the only viable way of being. Having Marxist roots, Sidanius was thinking mostly in terms of how wealthy elites push stories that convince everyone that they deserve to be rich and powerful and that the boat should not be rocked. One need not fixate on a Hard Left view of the world to understand that a wide variety of stories are used to uphold a way of life. Some of these stories are religious, some folkloric, some are novels or film scripts (acknowledge fiction, but still reinforcing ideas of what is normal). For Sidanius, these are all different ways of getting a sort of subliminal message across.

Other thinkers have also looked at different popular stories and analysed whether they supported listeners in developing strong or weak approaches to life. In the French folklorist Charles Perrault's 1697 rendition of *Red Riding Hood* his footnotes explicitly describe it as a tale warning young ladies not to be led astray by the silver-tongued roués of the royal court. In cultures where a woman's marriageable worth is largely dependent on her proclaimed virginity, it was important to hammer home such warnings to girls before the situation arose. Perrault also determined that the girl's outfit would be red, with earlier versions of the tale having placed no significance of the colour of what she wore.

In most Western societies these days a potential bride's sexual history is of little or no concern to most young men (or their parents). However, this does not mean the story has lost its significance, for there are subtle levels of meaning which emerge. Still of great concern to most parents is the fear that their naïve daughters might be led off the path of safety by a man who turns out to be a violent beast. The wolf here becomes a clear analogy for unrestrained, predatory male sexuality.

Angela Carter's radical reinterpretation of the story, *Company of Wolves*, picked up on another, more feminist interpretation of the tale – that the wolf not only represents a rapacious male sexuality but also the young girl's awakening to her own sexual appetites. The red hood becomes symbolic of menarche, symbolising not only her forthcoming fertility but plain old-fashioned lust. Victorians may have thought of erotic desire as predominantly masculine force (such that piano legs needed covering to avoid stimulating insatiable male desires), however, Carter is one of many who sees female sexuality as no less forceful and just as capable of over-riding common sense and leading a woman into doing things she might later regret. Whilst not a pagan herself, Carter's view of female sexuality certainly echoed ancient views of primal need.

Barbara G Walker was one of several pagan authors who saw a Jungian dynamic at play with Riding Hood, her mother and the old grandmother as representative of the Wiccan model of the goddess (though the stories long predate the formulation of those theological ideas). The wolf and the woodsman (who was a late introduction to the tale, probably added by the Brothers Grimm) are recast as the dual-aspected god of winter and summer respectively. Whatever your vision of deity, an argument could be made that the girl is taking a basket of offerings to the woodland temple of which the old woman might be the goddess or priestess. Perrault's advice to his female readers was to avoid listening to the beast. Some readers might think instead that the beast may be the only thing worth listening to, if the wolf represents the erotic or the unconscious forces.

The wolf as an embodiment of sexual potency has been explored within a few movies. The 2000 horror film *Ginger Snaps* picks up on Carter's literary idea of linking the sprouting of body hair and monthly transformations to female sexuality with a tale in which lycanthropy becomes analogous to puberty and the menstrual cycle. There are quite a few cultures in which menstruation is (mostly by men, but perhaps also by some women as well) as something rather monstrous and frightening. A very different film, the 1987 romantic comedy *Moonstruck*, makes several references to seeing the wolf in other people as a metaphor for seeing their lustful, wild side. Nicolas Cage's character, Ronny Cammareri, gets dumped by a fiancé after losing part of his hand in an industrial accident. His new love interest Loretta suggests that he was a wolf caught in a trap with this past relationship and that the loss of the hand was the wolf chewing its own paw off to get away. In this sense the lupine metaphor not only represents erotic force but also a primal ruthlessness that will do what it takes to attain freedom.

Just as Riding Hood's encounter tries to lure her off the straight and narrow socially approved path and into the wilderness, so the wolf has often served as an image of freedom away from the strictures of polite society. Both the 1990 film of *Dances with Wolves* and the book on which it is based feature a lone wolf that forms a bond with the protagonist John Dunbar. As Dunbar comes to question his loyalties to a corrupt army and the stultifying wider colonial society, the freedom of the wolf for which he yearns fuses in his mind with the lives of the Lakota Sioux that he also forms a lasting bond with. Without giving any spoilers, the wolf and the Lakota face parallel fates in the film. Not only does the wolf serve as an ethnic emblem within this narrative but is the manifestation of a natural, harmonious way of life. This romantic and positive view sits in direct contrast to the slavering, cannibalistic monsters of the horror films and earlier folktales.

Another popular European fairy story is that of the *Big Bad Wolf and the Three Little Pigs*. An 1886 version of this story involves three porcine brothers who each seek to build houses which the hungry wolf cannot get into. With the benefit of an impressive set of lungs, the wolf flattens the houses of straw and sticks, devouring the first two pigs in turn. The third pig is wise enough to build with brick, which thwarts the huffing and puffing. Modern renditions often end the story there, but older versions went on to recount various tricks played by the last pig on the wolf which finally ends with the wolf crawling down the brick chimney, landing in a cauldron and being cooked for the pig's dinner. There are assorted variations on the fairy tale in which the exact number of pigs and the chosen building materials differs, though the gist of the account remains essentially the same. There are also versions in which the builders are something other than pigs, and at least one version where the wolf is replaced with a fox.

The moral of the tale is clearly the importance of sensible planning against the vicissitudes of life, as embodied by the Big Bad. The wolf can largely be seen as emblematic of any number of potential problems that might beset a householder, the most obvious of which is famine. He is the proverbial wolf at the door which will tear down any unprepared house by starving the residents to death. Famine has become less of a global killer now than it was in the 1920s, but vast numbers of people around the world still suffer the deprivations of extreme hunger. The imagery of blowing the houses down, rather than tearing them apart with fang and claw as might be expected of a wolf, picks up on some worldwide traditions that howling can summon storms and wild winds.

The Brothers Grimm include a more positive representation, with the story of *The Good Wolf*. Here an elderly dog, Old Sultan, is booted out of the house by is ungrateful owners because they deem him too doddery to be an effective guard dog. The poor creature shares his woes with a wolf who stages an abduction of the baby, passing the unharmed infant on to Sultan to return as part of a faux rescue and so win back his place at the hearth. The wolf expects some kind of reward for his assistance, but sadly Sultan appears to have absorbed some of his owners' ingratitude and refuses to pay up. A fight ensues, but the two eventually declare a truce. The villains of this piece are clearly the owners and there is a definite resonance with another of the Grimm's stories, *Town Musicians of Bremen*, in which various farm animals are exploited and ill-used. The Chinese tale about the wolf in the Zhongshan forest, mentioned in a previous chapter, centres on this very experience, as voiced by a tree and a water buffalo. No doubt a good many loyal workers of the human variety will have sympathised with both Sultan and the Bremen beasts over the centuries, knowing full well what it is like to be worked to illness or decrepitude and then discarded without so much as a second thought. Little has changed in the 21st century.

For the Grimm's and whoever they collected the tale from, this wolf embodies cunning and ingenuity in playing the system. Old Sultan has a touch of false consciousness about him, in that he just wants to meekly return to his selfish owners rather than enjoy the wolf's freedom.

A number of stories centre on the contrast between the domesticated dog and the untamed wolf. Such tales often have a rather unresolved quality about them. The issue of which is better (a life of docile service but with regular meals and a warm hearth to sleep by, or one of freedom and passion but also often hunger and danger) is a dichotomy each person must resolve for themselves. Solzhenitsyn suggested the battle between good and evil runs through the heart; it might equally be said that the battle between freedom and security also does – and the costs of that conflict can be no less devastating, as humanity is likely to increasingly find as the 21st century rolls on.

The Greek slave Aesop purportedly won his freedom through his storytelling skills and left a considerable legacy of tales, several involving wolves. Probably the best known is *The Boy who Cried Wolf*, though really the wolf is hardly in it. An idle shepherd by finds he wins attention and praise by pretending to see a wolf harassing the sheep. His cries of *"wolf, wolf!"* pull a crowd but soon people get fed up of rushing out to find no emergency at all until they stop attending to him – whereupon the wolf really does appear and, without anyone willing to aid the boy, he gets eaten along with the sheep. As a morality tale there is a simple enough message about the dangers of raising false alarms and losing credibility (though plenty of politicians and campaigners carve long and lucrative careers wailing about disasters that never happen). A more subtle inference is that constantly referencing a problem almost conjures it into existence. In this tale the wolf is merely a representation of threat – he could be any kind of menace or danger that people worry about.

The story of the *Wolf and the Seven Kids* returns to the image of lupines as both cunning and greedy predators. A mother goat leaves her seven offspring at home with instructions not to open the door to strangers. The wolf soon sniffs out the tasty kids and, through guile, cons his way into the den where he eats six of them. The youngest hides and is soon found by the mother on her return, explaining what happens. The bloated wolf is sleeping it off in the goats' home, or in some versions, nearby. Either way, the mother finds him and slits open his belly to release her still-living children who have been neither chewed nor digested. Whilst at one level this plainly an advisory tale about silver-tongued strangers and obeying parents, it does have echoes to a much more graphic Greek tale. The primordial Cronus, intent on avoiding a prophecy by his own tyrannical father, swallows five of his children. The sixth child, Zeus, is hidden away and Cronus given a stone to consume. Eventually the overbearing father is forced to disgorge the swallowed children who appear to be no more harmed than the goats of Aesop's fable.

The story of Cronus might be about cannibalism, though a more plausible interpretation is a more psycho-spiritual one. Think of the oppressive force as not so much eating his children as so overshadowing and subsuming them that they cannot exist in their own right. There are families with just such overwhelming patriarchs or matriarchs that the children are barely visible at all outside the crushing egos of their parent. Equally a Jungian view would see these beings as all aspects of one psyche, in which one element so dominate all else that half the person remains woefully undeveloped and stunted until such time as the wolfish tyrant is overthrown and other parts of the Self can emerge.

The well-known Slavic fairy story of Ivan Tsarevich follows the popular folkloric pattern of having two rather useless older brothers and Ivan, the courageous youngest sibling. Shortening a long tale quite drastically, Ivan sets out on an adventure to please his royal father in finding a fabulous bird and comes to a talking stone at a crossroads. The stone instructs that two of the roads will involve death but does not say which is which. Whilst his elder brothers gave up when they heard the stone, Ivan plunges on and it is his horse which meets an untimely fate in the stomach of the Grey Wolf. The wolf offers to replace the horse as his steed, saving him from continuing his journey on foot.

Ivan, having joined the ranks of wolf-riders, finds that the Grey is also able to offer advice on how to complete his quest when he arrives at the castle where the firebird, which his father desires, now lives. Sadly Ivan is not sensible enough to follow the advice he is given and ends up needing to be bailed out of his predicament by the wolf. Thankfully the Grey is a forgiving soul and helps with the next stage of the adventure, rescuing a princess and even shapeshifting to impersonate her and fool a villainous king. The wolf later assumes the shape of a magical horse to allow another substitution to take place

Just when the story appears to be finished, rather like the *Fellowship of the Rings* movie, it continues on for several addenda. Thinking the tasks complete, Ivan and the Grey bid farewell and go their separate ways. Tragically Ivan and his princess are then jumped by the useless elder princes who murder their young brother and intimidate the maiden into silence. Whilst the murderous pair enjoy their royal privileges, the wolf finds the corpse and acquires magical waters that first restore the mangled body and then resurrect it. Finally the wolf-rider lopes into the palace, rescues his beloved and visits justice on his brothers (in one version, Grey eats them).

One of the best-known versions of this story was recorded by Alexander Afanasyev in *Russian Fairy Tales* (1855). He considered the folklore of his country to contain, *"more morality, truth and human love"* than Church sermons, so it is worth considering that, whilst Ivan's tale is basically a rollicking adventure, some semiotic significance can be read into the saga. Keeping the focus on the wolf, Jung argued that the speaking animals in such tales represent the instinctual mind that must be listened to and which guides the developing but still immature Self (i.e. Ivan Tsarevitch). The shape-changing substitutions offer an element of caveat emptor as the cunning wolf appears to fulfil Ivan's opponent's demands. That the Grey becomes a surrogate horse is reminiscent of the Irish myth of the boy Setanta temporarily taking the place of the massive guard dog of the blacksmith Culainn that he has killed. Depriving others of their necessities creates a duty to replace them. Both these stories feature restorative justice, an important concept in many earlier cultures which contrasts with the focus on punitive justice more prevalent in the modern world. There is a version where the wicked brothers are forced into servitude rather than eaten.

Chapter 10

When the Wolfsbane Blooms

On the off-chance that the reader is unfamiliar with the source of this chapter title, in the seminal 1941 Lon Chaney Jnr movie *The Wolfman*, the protagonist Lawrence Talbot returns to his ancestral home in Wales where assorted characters mutter the immortal lines dreamt up by scriptwriter Curt Siodmak:

> *Even a man who is pure in heart,*
> *and says his prayers by night;*
> *May become a wolf when the wolfsbane blooms*
> *and the autumn moon is bright.*

Outside of Hollywood, the wolfsbane normally blooms in spring and early summer. The wolfsbane plant derives its name from the use of the plant to tip arrows and other weapons by hunters in pursuit of wolves to whom it was believed to be especially poisonous. The Ancient Roman poet, Ovid, claimed that aconite, to use one of its other titles, grew from the saliva of Cerberus, the three-headed dog that guarded the gates of Hades. Some sources attribute the plant to Hecate, though the historicity of this is unclear.

German-born, Siodmak lived for a few years in Britain before emigrating to the States. Possibly his experience in Britain led him to set his script in Wales. As well as penning the above verse, Siodmak also invented the idea that those doomed to become the victim of a lycanthrope would have a pentagram appear on the palm of their hand. He is often regarded as having devised the idea that werewolves can only be killed by a weapon of silver (not necessarily a bullet). However, a German text from 1840 refers to a werewolf problem in 1640 being resolved by the use of silver bullets. It is possible that Siodmak was familiar with the text, or had at least heard the gist of this story being repeated and incorporated it into his script as the one-and-only way of dispatching a lycanthrope. Alternatively, and probably more likely, is that he read Bram Stoker's short story *Dracula's Guest* (1914) in which it is stated that werewolves must be shot by a sacred bullet – meaning one that has been blessed by a priest rather than necessarily made out of silver.

In one of the sequels to *The Wolfman* the verse was slightly amended so the last line read, *"and the moon is full and bright"* (possibly someone of horticultural bent had pointed out the issue with wolfsbane). This amendment would appear to be the root of the widespread notion that werewolves only shapeshift during a full moon. In earlier accounts, the shifting could occur at any time. These could be considered examples of fakelore – works of intentional fiction that become misinterpreted by the public as ancient traditions.

Previous chapters have included mention of werewolves in ancient polytheist literary works. The primary focus of this chapter will be on the common understanding of lycanthropy in the Christian era, chiefly by focusing on the legal prosecution of alleged werewolves though with also a few nods to the influence of cinematic monsters or contributing towards or inventing lore. The conviction that werewolves existed and were not the product of spooky stories told round the campfire was widespread, so much so that numerous people were put on trial and a fair few convicted for being werewolves. The earliest documented lycanthrope trials were held in 15th century Switzerland, though there may well be earlier cases for which no written records survive.

In 1521 Michel Verdun and Pierre Burgot were tried, condemned and burnt at the stake in Besançon, France for the alleged crimes of murdering and cannibalising a variety of people whilst in werewolf form. Under the interrogation techniques of the Inquisition, Burgot described how they had acquired shapeshifting power nearly twenty years earlier. A great storm had whipped up, scattering his flocks. Whilst trying to recover them he was approached by three unknown riders dressed in black. One offered him various protections and advantages in exchange for his service towards the riders' own master. Several days later Burgot was introduced to the master, who turned out to be the Devil using the name of Moyset. The pact was sealed and, for two years, he loyally served the infernal powers before relapsing into Christianity (presumably satanic servitude not being all it is cracked up to be).

Verdun appeared on the scene to draw Burgot back into diabolic duties with the added incentive of an unguent that would turn both men into lycanthropes. The first transformation took place deep in the forest at a gathering of other unnamed people (whether all male or mixed sex is not stated). They stripped naked and dances about with lit tapers before applying the mysterious salve. Having had their fun in wolf-shape a second salving took place (possibly with a different unguent rather than the original one) and they returned to humanity.

Assuming the story to be something other than torture-induced ravings, it is definitely suggestive. Quite a few werewolf trials make mention of salves and potions, which may well have contained entheogens to induce strange sensations – though it would be unusual if all participants had the same hallucinatory experiences. Who the Masters were leading these woodland ceremonies and what the purpose of them was is debatable. It is too easy to succumb to the romantic hope of late-lasting pagan wolf cults. The world has an abundance of peculiar sects and it may well have been something of much more recent origin and possessed of a different ideology entirely.

If all the other participants in the forest gathering were as murderous as Verdun and Burgot, the authorities would presumably have reported frenzied outbreaks of violent crimes all over France. Possibly the rest (if they existed) had quite different experiences with their ointment and did not kill or cannibalise anyone. The question of whether these two men were simply serial killers with wildly overactive imaginations, or if they were unstable participants in some much larger activity can only be speculation at this point in time.

The German farmer Peter Stumpp was nicknamed the Werewolf of Bedburg. At some point he had lost his left hand, though there is no surviving account of how that happened. He was brought to trial in 1598. He was accused of slaughtering fourteen children, one of them his own, and two adult women both of whom were pregnant. There is no supportive evidence to verify of these murders ever actually took place. He was alleged to have bumped these unfortunates off over many years for the pleasure of eating them (presumably whilst in wolf form). A number of trials made a direct connection between cannibalism and lycanthropy. The details of Stumpp's confession are quite horrific, but it must be borne in mind that this was gained under considerable torture. Whilst that does not guarantee that every word was false, people in great pain will clearly say anything to make it stop. The trial took an even more perverse turn when he admitted to incest with his teenage daughter who was then condemned to death alongside him.

Stumpp and his tragic daughter, plus a female companion, were executed in a grotesque manner on Halloween. Whilst that day has clear connotations for modern people, it is unlikely that the courts of 1598 chose it with any spectral intent in mind.

An interesting feature of the trial was Stumpp's account of how he became a werewolf. When still a youngster, he was presented with a magical belt by the Devil. When he wished to change shape, he would tie on the belt. The use of pieces of enchanted animal skin to engage in shapeshifting crops up around the world and may have its roots in memories of early shamanic rituals. By the 1500s the context had been mostly lost but the concept of mystical scraps of pelt persisted.

Merili Metsvahi (2015) outlines the wide extent of werewolf folklore and criminal trials in Livonia (part of modern-day Latvia). In one example from 1633 a witness called Gret gave testimony that Kanti Hans and his wife had turned into wolves, whilst a female accomplice had taken the shape of a bear. Metsvahi notes that Estonia has slightly more recorded stories about female werewolves than male, which is unusual given that most countries tend to regard it as a predominantly masculine phenomenon. An interesting feature of Estonian lore picked out by Metsvahi is that potential victims of a werewolf can save themselves by calling out his or her name, which pulls the shapeshifter back into their human form. This is, of course, reliant on the victim actually knowing who the person is underneath their hairy pelt. In some respects this is reminiscent of the Egyptian idea of the sacred name, the *ren*, which captures the very essence of Being and, by being spoken, brings that presence into the world. this is not to suggest any cultural connections between Egypt and Estonia, only that certain philosophical concepts recur the world over. One might well speculate that this is because they are fundamentally true.

The same author goes on to distinguish between two forms of lycanthrope in Estonian lore – the voluntary and involuntary. Whilst the wilful shapeshifter can be recalled to humanity through the speaking of names, the person who has been forced into lycanthropy (usually by a curse) can be brought out of it by the proffering of bread. This might be partially an image of domesticity and the return to the companionship of humanity (the French origin of the word companionship comes from the words for breaking bread – the same linguistic link does not appear to be true of the respective Estonian words, so this may be stretching a point somewhat), but also likely alludes to the communion wafer and the return to the Christian fold as sheep rather than wolf.

An element of class tension emerges in a portion of Estonian werewolf lore, which Metsvahi associates with historical problems produced by the native population being mostly relegated to impoverished peasants whilst the landowning elite were of Germanic origin. To some extent a British parallel can be drawn here if we look at the Robin Hood legends. Whilst there is no suggestion that the Hooded Man was ever a werewolf, he was labelled a wolfshead – an outlaw – and lived with his Merrie Men who were somewhat akin to a loyal pack. In early ballads and tales, Robin is a Saxon of humble stock (late tales often revise this to his being a displaced Normal lordling). The fat bishops and corrupt aristocrats whom the Merrie Men rob and humiliate are almost entirely from the Norman occupiers. In taking to the life of a dangerous wolf in the forest with his fierce pack, Robin strikes out against corrupt tyrants who make the peasants' lives a misery. A similar argument can be made about the Estonian werewolves making their discontent known.

In Livonia in 1651, a teenager known simply as Hans was hauled into court at Idavere to face charges of lycanthropy. Almost immediately he offered up a seemingly free confession (records make no mention of his being torture) that he had had a most peculiar encounter at the age of sixteen. An unnamed man dressed in black had approached him and bitten him. Afterwards he became a werewolf and had predated upon others, though no evidence as to any actual deaths appears to have been offered. He announced that he felt more like a savage beast than a civilised human. The notion that some forms of lycanthropy were linked to dissociative mental states seems to have been acknowledge by the court, because the judge questioned whether the transformation was actual or more of a dream state. The judge convicted him and sentenced him to death upon hearing Hans describe being bitten by a dog whilst in wolf-form and still having the wound after returning to humanity. It is more than likely that the lad was intellectually challenged to place his own life so freely in the executioner's hands and it would be easy to dismiss the confession as an adolescent fantasy. However, the mention of the man dressed in black is one that recurs in other trials in other countries. It may be that he had heard this as a popular fireside tale and simply repeated it to the judge, but it is curious nonetheless.

The trial of another youngster, Jean Grenier, had taken place in Landes, France several decades earlier in 1603. An impoverished, half-starved lad of roughly thirteen years old had frightened a group of girls during a picnic. Dragged before the courts he also offered a garrulous confession without prompting of torture. He had bragged to the girls and later to the judge that he was a werewolf who had eaten a variety of animals and young children. He was able to give dates and locations of attacks which did indeed correlate with disappearances. Unhinged claims of cannibalism and magical powers were, in some respects, the least surprising part of this court case. What is far harder to explain is the behaviour of the judge, Pierre de Lancre. Working on the Bordeaux court circuit, he oversaw the brutal witch trials of Labourd and wrote about satanic shenanigans with a level of prurient credulity that suggests a glassy-eyed level of belief in his own self-righteous campaign against imaginary evils. As Pearl (1999) marks, de Lancre was by no means unusual or especially fanatical in his beliefs at the time. Whilst scepticism was growing in some quarters, de Lancre's absolute conviction in the existence of demonic orgies and the supernatural powers of devil worshippers was share by the majority of educated people as well as the peasantry.

Where a significant echo between Jean and Hans can be found is in the boy's account of how he became a werewolf. Grenier said that some years earlier a neighbour had taken him deep into the local woods where they met with a group of unnamed men. Here they waited until the Master of the Forest appeared, described ambiguously as either a black man or a man dressed in black, and presented them with a jar of ointment and a wolf pelt. The story also echoes that of Verdun and Burgot from eight decades earlier. The illiterate shepherd boy would not have been able to read any of those trial accounts, but a small possibility exists that he could have heard idle chatter about the murders of so many years previous. That said, Landes and Besançon are about 500 miles apart so it is debatable how far the story might have travelled.

Despite the intensity of his outlook, the judge listened to Grenier's claims of cannibalism, brutality, and magic with a surprising level of compassion and proclaimed that the lad was clearly deluded and had what these days would be referred to as severe learning difficulties. Why he did not believe the boy but later believed practically every outlandish confession at the witch trials is unclear, but instead of the usual horrific punishments meted out to those who dabbled in dark magic, he sentenced Grenier to be kept under effective house arrest at a monastery for the remainder of his life. Seven years later the judge paid him a visit, where Grenier repeated his tale and seemed little changed. The only additions were the claim that the mysterious man from the forest had tried to visit him at the monastery but been repelled. Grenier died around the age of twenty from unknown causes.

As with the unfortunate Hans several decades later, the question remains as to whether these stories were entirely the product of overheated imaginations or if there were elements of truth. The mention by Grenier of an ointment could suggest some hallucinogenic salve presented to him by someone with sufficient intelligence to make it, though why they would give it to a boy of that age is anyone's guess. If he was indeed drawn to the forest by a neighbour, it could have been for some deeply unpleasant sexual purpose but a possibility remains of some kind of cultic activity in which the black figure inducted Grenier into some sort of esoteric activity involving hallucinogens. It is to be hoped that murder and mayhem were not the intended results of using the unguent, but maybe Grenier's mental capacities were greatly overestimated?

Quite a few witch trials over the centuries made mention of a Man in Black, a mysterious officer of the coven who acted as go-between with other covens. Many modern covens keep up the tradition of having such a role today. Trial records and folktales often present this figure as basically being the Devil rather than a mortal devotee. Historical reviews by Pumfrey (2003), Leeson & Russ (2017) and others have speculated that anti-Catholicism in Protestant countries fuelled many notions about witchcraft. Notions of a black-robed man engaged in strange rituals in lonely spots might owe more to fervid imaginings about Catholic priests meeting to hold outlawed Masses than to any pagan, much less satanic, gatherings. It needs to be borne in mind that, to many hard-line Puritans of centuries past, Catholicism was basically devil worship by another name. In Catholic countries such as France, this argument fails to account for what people like Jean Grenier might have experienced in the forest.

Despite the recurrent claims at different trials of esoteric gatherings distributing magical ointments, it is too great a leap to suggest that wolf cults might have been active in 17th century rural France (or other countries), though it does make for a good film plot or future novel!

A far more vivid source of speculative claims than either Grenier or Hans comes from the 1692 Livonian trial of an elderly man called Thiess of Kaltenbrun. A great deal was made of this court case by the Italian historian Carlo Ginzburg (1966). In a rather strange turn of events, Thiess was required to give evidence in a case of robbery but announced to the judges, apropos of very little it would seem, that he was a lycanthrope. This came as scant surprise to his neighbours, who had long suspected it. Without prompting of torture or other intimidations, the old man gave a convoluted explanation of the secret world of werewolves and other supernatural beings. Paranormal society was divided between workers of benevolent magic and their malign counterparts. Thiess and his fellow werewolves were on the side of the good guys, using their magical powers to battle the forces of evil that would spread misery in the world of ordinary mortals given half a chance. The lycanthrope described how the wolves would journey down into Hell three times a year: Pentecost (which falls fifty days after Easter Sunday), St John's Day (24th June), and St Lucia's Day (13th December). Prior to retiring from active magical service, Thiess said he had owned a wolf pelt the donning of which enabled him to shapeshift. Prior to making the journey to Hell, the werewolves would glut themselves on local farm animals, perhaps regarding this as a sort of down payment for services to be rendered. Having defeated the servants of Satan, the werewolves would rescue the worldly goods (mostly farm produce) which they had stolen and return them to the various farmers.

Despite his impassioned claims that werewolves were devoted to God and opposed the Devil, the judges found him guilty. Unusually Thiess was not executed, but sentenced to be flogged (though as he was eighty years old at the time, this might well have proved fatal anyway). He was afterwards banished, disappearing from the pages of history.

Ginzburg makes a comparison between Thiess' story and that told of the Italian *benandanti* cult, members of which came to wider attention in various trials over the course of a century, starting in 1575. Aside from the lack of werewolves in the Italian story, the battle of magical enemies for the good of the populace remains really quite similar. Ginzburg and others, such as Klaniczay (1990), argue that this is an example of ancient pagan rites surviving long into the Christian era. Others have dismissed this as a romantic whimsy and suggested the roots are much more recent and that such tales embody ongoing ideas of the conflict between summer and winter, Christ and the Devil, or generic notions of order and chaos. Whatever the case, there are certainly fascinating subcultures existing underneath mainstream religious views. That Livonian werewolves should serve the forces of goodness (despite devouring some livestock every now and then) is a pleasant relief from the usual tales of unrelenting horror. Whilst Thiess could be dismissed as simply mad, it may well be that his view of wolves reflects a much older Livonian outlook, reaching back before the area Christianised and came to assume that the wolf must be the implacable enemy of Christ the Good Shepherd.

The idea that poor old Thiess might have been part of some secretive ritualistic group does have a deliciously romantic appeal to it. If we entertain the idea that the benevolent wizards existed then it implies that the diabolical forces, one of whom was a farmer who had previously broken Thiess' nose in an altercation, might also have banded together. There are certainly numerous secretive organisations with strange ceremonies in the world today, so it would be nice to think that at least some of them are trying to be of benefit to the world rather than the usual array of ideological fanatics and self-indulgent debauchees.

For three years, starting in 1764, part of France was terrorised by what became known as the Beast of Gévaudon. Due to unreliability of records, accounts of exactly how many people died vary wildly between 60 and 500 with a raft more left with non-fatal injuries. Some of these stories may have been completely fictitious, dreamt up by self-publicists wanting to sell a good story. The attacks took place over quite a wide area and the strong possibility remains that there may have been more than one Beast. Several people claimed to have killed the

Beast and if there was more than one dangerous animal at large, then perhaps they were all telling the truth after a fashion. The first victim to survive, Valet, described the creature as being very much like a wolf without actually being one. This has led to a great deal of speculation as to quite what the animal was, whether simply a very large or even malformed wolf through to a hyena or even a big cat – this was the solution offered by the 2001 French film *Brotherhood of the Wolf*, where it is a lion in rather strange armour that is being used by its handler to spread terror and political discord. Unfortunately the Beast has cast a long shadow and contributed to the widespread view that wolves are extremely dangerous. As Jean Baudrillard noted, fictional works can have greater influence than lived reality.

Afterword

For those readers who are strongly drawn towards the Wolf Spirit, whether this is a new exploration or a longstanding commitment, it is worth reflecting that bonding to spirit also leads to responsibilities in the material world. Whilst this is true of any kind of totemic association (to use that term in a very loose manner), it is especially so where an animal is at significant risk. Whilst wolves are returning to some areas of the world where they had previously been driven to extinction, the overall numbers are still very low and there are too many people doing their best to reduce it yet further.

A gift begets a gift, so those who gain some benefits from the presence of Wolf Spirits could return the benevolence in a variety of ways but a key one is improving the life chances of incarnate wolves. There are a number of charities around the world which look after wolves in wildlife reserves, educate the public about the positive contributions made by wolves to the environment, or support wolves in the wild through preserving their ecosystems. Such organisations can be aided through volunteering time, skills, donating money or goods etc.

Many readers will doubtless already be doing so, but others who are at the start of finding spiritual companionship are encouraged to give back in whatever ways they feel to be viable. Some readers may live in countries which have wild wolf populations and could potentially journey out into isolated spots where they might catch a glimpse of a passing wolf, or more likely be able to hear them calling to each other. Those readers who live in parts of the world where wolves have been eradicated from the wild might only be able to have such an experience via zoos, safari parks, or wildlife preserves. There are assorted ethical problems with such places, particularly if they are badly run, but maybe some readers will be in a position to assist achieving positive change in the less admirable establishments.

One topic that produces often heated debate is the question of using body parts in ritual. Numerous cultures both ancient and modern have deployed feathers, fur, horns, bones, and suchlike in ritualistic manners as well as in more prosaic forms (such as fashion or scientifically dubious medicine). Chancing upon stray feathers or shed antlers is a wonderful boon and causes no harm to the creatures that have lost them. The same is true of happening upon the bones of something that was dead long before – though caution is advised, partly for medical reasons (in case whatever caused the death remains an active risk) and partly for spiritual ones. If the creature died in pain and distress there may be a lingering aura ill-suited to magical usage. It is recommended that the reader consult with the spirit of the departed animal, through meditation of whatever technique works best for you, to seek permission to take a bone or two.

Ethical issues to one side, the discussion of body parts also has to consider what one does with them having acquired them. The author has friends who are osteophiles – a word made up on the spur of the moment to describe collectors of bones who do not really do anything with the bones per se (mostly skulls), but just love looking at them in much the same way that a philologist pours over books of stamps. A great many pagans (and probably others) could be described as talismaniacs, in that their homes are crushed beneath the weight not only of found bones but unusual stones, curious-shaped bits of driftwood, and any number of other objects that were jammed into pockets whilst perambulating with a magpie instinct for the magical and bizarre. Rarely, if ever, do they actually deploy such objects for occult purposes. They are horded to be admired, and possibly to drive spouses to desperation, rather than for a specific intent.

Some will, of course, have more definite intent in mind and may use the detritus of animal life to create shamanic rattles, decorate drums, ritual robes, create amulets to gift or sell, and a dozen other possible ends. As per the point earlier, it is worth consulting with the spirit of the animal in question to see if it is willing to be used to such an end. We could link this to philosophical notions such as German philosopher Immanuel Kant's excellent advice that the truly decent person should treat others (he was mainly talking of fellow humans, but this can be extended to a much wider field) as Ends-in-Themselves rather than using and exploiting them as merely Means-to-an-End. Much of what is wrong in human societies over the millennia can be tracked back to treating others as merely objects to be used and discarded. Asking for permission should be a genuine act rather than a case of going through the motions – in other words, ask with the realisation that the answer might well be negative, whereupon the body part must be left alone.

Getting hold of lupine remains will rather more of a challenge for some than others, depending on where a person lives in the world. A chanced-upon tooth or clump of fur will pose fewer ethical concerns than buying a full pelt that has come from a wolf that has been hunted. There are nature reserves where culling is used to manage pack size or euthanise unwell or injured wolves. There are also sports hunters who will sell on bits of their kills for profit. The moral complications with this are obvious and the reader must decide for themselves if the item can be used for ceremonial ends or if the route by which it has left the world has tainted the part beyond use. Not everyone, ancient pagans included, has been so squeamish about acquisitions and, indeed, some cultures emphasise the right of the victor to do as they please with the spoils of a hunt or a battle. Sometimes subjugating a disgruntled spirit into service has been portrayed as a display of magical strength rather than perceived as an act of horrible abuse.

Having listed a few possible uses earlier, the precise body part might dictate the use. A tooth might lend itself more to defensive magic or to aid in hunting, whilst a tail might be far better suited to communicative magic, or a skull to the enhancement of cunning and strategy.

Reaching the end of the book, it will be clear (if it was not already) that wolves have been understood in a rich and diverse array of ways – sometimes lauded as wise teachers and icons of pack loyalty, at other junctures feared as slavering and ferocious threats to existence, embodiments of chaos and destruction. The reader who intends to engage ritually with the spirit of wolf (whether aided by body parts or not) needs to be clear in their own mind, informed by their own cultural heritage or those of cultures which they have embraced, as to quite who and what they wish to deal with. This Afterword has sought to emphasise that deal is the operative word. As the Romans were wont to say when making ceremonial offerings, *Do ut des* (I give that you may give). Wolves do not leave empty-bellied, if you do not willingly feed them their due, they will take a few tasty morsels of their own choice. Know what you want, know what you will offer in exchange, and know that wolves talk. All that howling is as much gossip as it is the sweet music of the children of the night. Reputations for generosity or stinginess get round.

References

Abu'l-Mundhir Khaleel ibn Ibraaheem Ameen (2005). *The Jinn and Human Sickness: Remedies in the Light of the Qur'an and Sunah*. Riyadh, Darussalam.

Afanasyec, A. (2013). *Russian Fairy Tales*. The Planet (illustrated edition).

Anthes, R. (1974). D*ie Berichte des Neferhotep und des Ichernofret über das Osirisfest in Abydos (The reports of Neferhotep and Ichernofret about the Osiris Festival in Abydos)*, in Müller, W. (ed.), Festschrift zur 150 Jahrigen Bestehen des Berliner Ägyptischen Museum, Mitteilungenaus der Ägyptischen Sammlung 8, Berlin, Akademie Verlag, 15–49.

Benedict, R. (1989). *The Chrysanthemum and the Sword*. USA: Houghton Mifflin.

Bernhardt-House, P. (2017). *Binding the Wolf, Leashing the Hound: Canid Eschatologies in Irish and Norse Myth*. Studia Celtica Fennica.

Blaiklock, E. M. (ed) et al (1085). *The Little Flowers of St Francis*. London: Hodder & Stoughton Religious.

Boas, F. & Rink, H. (1889). *Eskimo Tales and Songs*. Journal for American Folklore, 2 (5): 123–131.

Boyle, E. & Hayden, D. (ed.) (2014). 'On the Wonders of Ireland: Translation and Adaptation', in *Authorities and Adaptations: The Reworking and Transmission of Textual Sources in Medieval Ireland* (Dublin: Dublin Institute for Advanced Studies), pp. 233-61.

Čajkanović, V. (1994). *Stara srpska religija i mitologija* (Old Serbian Religion and Mythology). Belgrade: Serbian Literary Cooperative.

Cambrensis, G. & Forester, T. (trans.) (2000). *The Topography of Ireland*. Cambridge: In Parentheses Publications.

Cook, A. B. (1914). *Zeus: A Study in Ancient Religion*. Cambridge: Cambridge University Press.

Dooley, A. & Roe, H. (1999). *Tales of the elders of Ireland*. Oxford: Oxford University Press.

Dowling, C. (1981). *The Cinderella Complex*. New York: Simon and Schuster.

Evans, L. (2011). The Shedshed of Wepwawet: An Artistic and Behavioural Interpretation. Journal of Egyptian Archaeology.

Fortune, D. (2001). *Psychic Self-Defence*. Boston: Weiser Books.

Fuller, D. J. (2012). Interview: Dr Phillip Bernhardt-House on Celtic Werewolves. http://www.davidjonfuller.com/2012/10/17/interview-dr-phillip-bernhardt-house-on-celtic-werewolves/

Ginzburg, C. (1983). *The Night Battles: Witchcraft and Agrarian Cults in the Sixteenth and Seventeenth Centuries*. Baltimore: Johns Hopkins University Press.

Gundarsson, K. (1993). *Teutonic Religion*. USA: Llewellyn Publications.

Hirono, H. & Nako, O. (2008). *Sebu to Okami no Yakusoku [A Promise of Sebu and Wolf]*. Foundation for Research and Promotion of Ainu Culture.

Kipling, R. (2018). *The Jungle Book*. London: Wordsworth Editions.

Klaniczay, G. (1990). *The Uses of Supernatural Power. The Transformations of the Popular Religion in Medieval and Early Modern Europe*. Cambridge: Polity Press.

Langer, J. (2018). *The Wolf's Jaw: An Astronomical Interpretation of Ragnarök*. Archaeoastronomy and Ancient Technologie, 6(1), 1-20.

Larson, L. M. (trans.) (1917). *The King's Mirror*. American-Scandinavian Foundation.

Leeson, P. & Russ, J. (2017). *Witch Trials*. The Economic Journal, 128 (August), 2066–2105.

Livy, T. (trans. Spillan, D.) (1854). *The History of Rome, books 01 – 08*. Project Gutenberg.

Maruyama, N. (2014). Wolves Save Japan! Ecosystem Role and Need for Resurrection. Tokyo: Baishuishe.

Mencej, M. (2001). *Master of Wolves in Slavic Mythology*. Ljubljana: Faculty of Arts.

Metsvahi, M. (2015). *Estonian werewolf legends collected from the island of Saaremaa,* in Priest, H. (ed.). *She-wolf: a cultural history of female werewolves.* Manchester: Manchester University Press, pp. 24-40.

Pearl, J. L. (1999). *The Crime of Crimes: Demonology and Politics in France 1560–1620.* Wilfrid Laurier University Press.

Peterson, B. (2013). *The Song The Owl God Sang: The collected Ainu legends of Chiri Yukie* BJS Books.

Petronius (ed. Walsh, P. G.) (2009). *The Satyricon.* Oxford: Oxford University Press.

Pluskowski. A. G. (2004). *Lupine apocalypse: the wolf in pagan and Christian cosmology in medieval Britain and Scandinavia.* In: Cosmos 17, 2001. pp. 113-131.

Pumfrey, S. A. (2002). *The Lancaster Witches: Histories and Stories.* Manchester: Manchester University Press.

Ratcliffe, D. (1997). *The Raven.* London: Poyser.

Rohrich, L. & Tokofsky, P. (trans.) (1991). *Folktales and Reality.* Indiana: Indiana University Press.

Smith, B. (2021). *The real story behind the Shetland wulver.* Shetland Museum Archives.

Speidel, M. (2004). *Ancient Germanic Warriors: Warrior Styles from Trajan's Column to Icelandic Sagas,* London: Routledge.

Strechie, M. (2014). *The Myth/Symbol of the Wolf in Sparta, Dacia and Rome.* Sapientia et scientia. In honorem Luciae Wald, Bucureşti, Editura, pp. 292-299.

Vegh, Z. (2009). *Counting the Dead – Some Remarks on the Haker-Festival.* Current Research in Egyptology 2009, Proceedings of the 10th Annual Symposium. Oxbow Books.

References

Venclová, N. (2002). *The Venerable Bede, druidic tonsure and archaeology.* Antiquity, 76(292), 458-471 Uniuversităţii din Bucureşti, 2014, 372 p., pp. 292-29.

Bibliography

Arbuthnot, S. (editor) (2006). *Coir Anmann*. London, Irish Texts Society.

Baring-Gould, S. (1865). *Book of Werewolves*. London: Smith, Elder & Co.

Binchy, D. A. (1975). *Irish History and Irish Law*. *Studia Hibernica* (15): 7–36.

Bomford, L. (1993). *The Complete Wolf*. London, Boxtree.

Carter, A. (1995). *The Bloody Chamber*. Croydon: Vintage.

Douglas, A. (1992). *The Beast Within*. London, Chapmans.

Dronke, U. (1997). *The Poetic Edda* Volume II *Mythological Poems*. Oxford: Clarendon Press.

Ellis, S. (2011). *Wolves*. Bath, Parragon.

Fiennes, R. (1976). *The Order of Wolves*. New York, Bobbs-Merrill Company.

Faulkes, A. (ed.) (2008). *Edda*, Norse text and English notes. Everyman Series, London: W&N.

Grimm, J & Grimm W. (2013). *Fairy Tales from the Brothers Grimm*. London: Puffin Books.

Howes, R. C. (trans.) (1973). *The Tale of the Campaign of Igor*. USA: W W Norton.

Kelly, F. (1988). *A Guide to Early Irish Law*. Early Irish Law Series 3. Dublin: DIAS.

McCone, K. (1986). *Werewolves, cyclopes, díberga and fíanna: juvenile delinquency in early Ireland*. Cambridge Medieval Celtic Studies 12 (Winter).

Perrault, C & Mansion, J. E. (trans.) (1969). *Perrault's Fairy Tales*. Dover; Dover Publications.

Plas, P. (2010). *Wolves and Death: The Thanatological Meaning of the Wolf in Western South Slavic Traditional Culture*. Croatian Journal for Ethnology and Folklore.

Priest, H. (editor) (2015). *She-wolf, a Cultural History of Female Werewolves.* Manchester, Manchester University Press.

Rehnmark, E. (2000). *Neither God nor Devil.* San Francisco, Pomegranate.

Simek, R. (1993). *Dictionary of Northern Mythology.* Rochester, NY, Boydell & Brewer.

Steiger, B. (1999). *The Werewolf Book.* London, Visible Ink Press.

Walker, B G. (1996). *Feminist Fairytales.* HarperCollins INC International Concepts.

Woodward, I. (1979). *The Werewolf Delusion.* London, Paddington Press.

MOON BOOKS
PAGANISM & SHAMANISM

What is Paganism? A religion, a spirituality, an alternative belief system, nature worship? You can fi nd support for all these definitions (and many more) in dictionaries, encyclopaedias, and text books of religion, but subscribe to any one and the truth will evade you. Above all Paganism is a creative pursuit, an encounter with reality, an exploration of meaning and an expression of the soul. Druids, Heathens, Wiccans and others, all contribute their insights and literary riches to the Pagan tradition. Moon Books invites you to begin or to deepen your own encounter, right here, right now.

If you have enjoyed this book, why not tell other readers by posting a review on your preferred book site.

Bestsellers from Moon Books
Pagan Portals Series

The Morrigan
Meeting the Great Queens
Morgan Daimler
Ancient and enigmatic, the Morrigan reaches out to us.
On shadowed wings and in raven's call, meet the ancient Irish
goddess of war, battle, prophecy, death, sovereignty, and magic.
Paperback: 978-1-78279-833-0 ebook: 978-1-78279-834-7

The Awen Alone
Walking the Path of the Solitary Druid
Joanna van der Hoeven
An introductory guide for the solitary Druid, The Awen Alone will
accompany you as you explore, and seek out your own place
within the natural world.
Paperback: 978-1-78279-547-6 ebook: 978-1-78279-546-9

Moon Magic
Rachel Patterson
An introduction to working with the phases of the Moon,
what they are and how to live in harmony with the lunar
year and to utilise all the magical powers it provides.
Paperback: 978-1-78279-281-9 ebook: 978-1-78279-282-6

Hekate
A Devotional
Vivienne Moss
Hekate, Queen of Witches and the Shadow-Lands, haunts the pages
of this devotional bringing magic and enchantment into your lives.
Paperback: 978-1-78535-161-7 ebook: 978-1-78535-162-4

Readers of ebooks can buy or view any of these bestsellers by clicking on the live link in the title. Most titles are published in paperback and as an ebook. Paperbacks are available in traditional bookshops. Both print and ebook formats are available online.

Find more titles and sign up to our readers' newsletter:
johnhuntpublishing.com/paganism

For video content, author interviews and more, please subscribe to our YouTube channel.

MoonBooksPublishing

Follow us on social media for book news, promotions and more:

Facebook: Moon Books Publishing

Instagram: @moonbooksjhp

Twitter: @MoonBooksJHP

Tik Tok: @moonbooksjhp